THE TENNIS PARENT'S BIBLE:

A Comprehensive Survival Guide to Becoming a World Class Tennis Parent (or Coach)

By

Frank Giampaolo

Also Available by Frank:

CHAMPIONSHIP TENNIS
(Human Kinetics Worldwide Publishing)

The Mental Emotional Tennis Work Book:
International Player Evaluation

The Mental Emotional Tennis Work Book:
Blunders and Cures

The Mental Emotional Tennis Work Book:
Insights & Antidotes

The Mental Emotional Tennis Work Book:
Protocols of Winning

The Mental Emotional Tennis Work Book:
Match Chart Collection

The Mental Emotional Tennis Work Book
Match Day Preparation

The Mental Emotional Tennis Work Book:
How to Attract a College Scholarship

Web Sites:
http://www.tennisparentsolutions.com
http://www.thetennisparentsbible.com

Facebook:
http://facebook.com/tennisbible.giampaolo@gmail.com

Copyright 2010

INDUSTRY PROFESSIONAL TESTIMONIALS

"The Tennis Parent's Bible is a must read for any competitive tennis family. This book should be on each parent's night stand and in every coach's racket bag. Frank has truly captured what the parent of an aspiring athlete needs to know."

Craig Tiley, Tournament Director Australian Open, Director of Tennis, Tennis Australia

"Frank is quickly becoming one of the games most respected and influential teachers. As the coach of a top 5 WTA player, I recommend The Tennis Parent's Bible to anyone serious about developing a champion."

Sam Sumyk, Coach of Victoria Azarenka # 4 on the WTA World Tour

"Frank is a skilled lecturer & a top teacher. Now as an author, Frank has written one of the most important developmental books I've seen in my 60 years of teaching. This should be required reading for every inspiring parent, player or coach!"

Vic Braden, The Vic Braden Tennis College

"There are few people who have earned as much respect in the tennis world. Frank is a positive visionary."

Dick Gould, Stanford University (The most successful coach in college tennis history.)

"A world class book written by a world class coach. This is a book that every junior parent needs to read."

Peter Smith USC Men's Tennis Coach, Current 3-Time National Champions

"Frank is one of the most knowledgeable tennis coaches in the country. He has written, in my professional opinion, the best and most comprehensive tennis book for parents that I've read in my 55 –year tennis career."

Desmond Oon, Ph.D., Former Davis Cup Coach (Republic of Singapore), Author, Master Pro USPTA

"I'm always proud to see great USPTA members take tennis teaching to the next level. Frank seems to excel at everything he does."

Tim Heckler, CEO, United States Professional Tennis Association

"Frank's work is positive, constructive, enlightening, liberating, and best of all fun."

Billy Martin, UCLA Men's Tennis Coach

PARENTAL/PLAYER TESTIMONIALS

"Having recently worked in Australia with my 9 years old son, Frank was able to leave a legacy of knowledge which has resulted in my son being able to quickly and effectively analyze an opponent and apply winning strategies. The results were amazing and instantaneous. We can't wait to spend more time with Frank. Australia needs more coaches like Frank. No other coach has had such an impact on Marcus in such a short period of time."

George Stathos, (Parent of Marcus Stathos Boys 10's), Melbourne, Australia

"Frank's weekend workshop was so illuminating it probably changed our lives! The sessions gave us the tools we needed as parents to guide our daughter through the national levels. Frank really made a lasting impression on our little girl."

Keira Northaft, Tempe, Arizona (Delaney Northaft Girls 10's, #1 Southwest Section)

"Frank has been instrumental in my son's development. His overall tennis knowledge is second to none. There is no problem he can't solve on the tennis court. He has been a great asset for us!"

Gary & Lucy Karagezian, Burbank, California (Arthur Karagezian, boys 16's, #6 Sectional Ranking, #37 National Ranking)

"Frank has great knowledge of both the mental & physical parts of the game that I take with me into every match."

Greg Scott, Pacific Palisades, California (boys 16's, #3 Sectional Ranking, top 25 National Ranking)

"Molly's success in tennis is due to the coaching she receives from Frank. In particular, Frank has taught her how to construct points and develop strategies to beat different styles of opponents. He also makes the long hours of training enjoyable. When Molly's coming home from College, Frank is one of the first people she calls."

Jim & Cindy Scott , Coto De Caza, California (Molly Scott #1 SCTA, WTA player, First Team all-Ivy League, Dartmouth College)

"When it comes time to find a coach to teach the mental/emotional sides of the game, the list of qualified coaches becomes amazingly short. We are extremely fortunate to have found Frank!"

Glenn & Cheryl Daynes, Rancho Santa Margareta, Ca. (Gannon Daynes Boys 14's #9 Sectional Ranking, #40 National Ranking)

"With Frank's humor, knowledge and years of experience a perfect storm is created! A thinking, fast pace session that is so beneficial and fun! "

Dave & Linda Labarres, Alberta, Canada (Garrett's Labarre Boys 18's, # 1 Alberta, Canada Matt Labarre, Boys 14's ,#4 Alberta, Canada)

"Absolutely the best motivator in the business." Frank's technical expertise, knowledge of the game and extreme enthusiasm puts him head and tails above the rest."

Cindy Hayley, Houston Texas (Abby Hayley, Top 20 in Texas, Fresno State)

"I've had the opportunity to work with most of the best coaches in the United States. Nobody gets results like Frank."

Sarah Fansler, Newport Beach, California (10 National Singles Titles, WTA tour, U.S. Open, #1 at USC)

"We have worked with some of the top coaches in England and Florida. We value Frank's approach over any of the elite academies."

Muri Nathan, Rancho Santa Margareta, California (Ahdiv Nathan, Boys 16's International Player)

TAKING IT TO THE NEXT LEVEL

Litchfield Park, Arizona July 20th, 2009

Regarding: Tennis Parents Workshops and Mental/Emotional Tennis Workshops

Our program Wigwam Tennis has greatly benefited from Frank Giampaolo's Tennis Parent's Workshops. We hosted one at the Wigwam Resort in May 2007 during which over 20 families participated. In April 2009 we traveled with the group of 15 families to Frank's facility in Southern California.

Parents' education programs offered by Frank are absolutely essential to player development. Addressing this link in the developmental chain is of utmost importance since the parents spent the most time with the players and they are still #1 source of information, feedback and support to the player. Increasing knowledge base among parents will have direct positive impact on quality of player development in U.S.

Frank is one of the best experts in the game of tennis. His knowledge of players and parents as well as overall in depth knowledge of the game and the process of tennis skill acquisition make him most suitable to conduct such workshops at the national scale.

Within our program the feedback after workshops has been incredible. Workshops with Frank facilitated coaches-parents communications and relationships. Frank skillfully and sensitively balances parent, coach and player triangle, helping all 3 links function more effectively without causing frictions.

It would be of great benefit to player development in the U.S. to involve Frank with parents' education programs on the national scale.

Robert Wojcik Program Director, Wigwam Tennis/Delray Tennis Center

TABLE OF CONTENTS

Overlooking The Pain Principle
Assuming That Tennis Speed is Only Foot Speed

INTELLIGENT TRAINING Blunders
Not Having an Entourage
Being Oblivious to Periodization
Neglecting Smart Work
Encouraging "One Set Wonders"
Putting Them in the Crowd to Get Ahead of the Crowd
Believing Weekly Lessons are Enough
Going into Battle Unprepared

PART FOUR: Common Questions & Solutions

ORGANIZATIONAL ISSUES
How do we find the right professional?
The XYZ tennis academy has offered us a scholarship?
Mental & Emotional myths of junior competition?
What does a top player's weekly schedule look like?
How do we plan our child's tournament schedule?
In scheduling practice sets, what should my daughter focus on?
My mom only wants me to play with better players, then goes psycho when I lose. Is that right?
Even after a practice set, my dad asks me "Did you win?"
Should my son copy Nadal?
How come so many great juniors never make it?

MAKING WISER CHOICES
How should my son handle cheaters?
How do we help our son overcome his on court-anger?
How do we spot tennis burn out?
Is high school tennis right for my son?
My son says I'm negative. How do I push…nicely?
My husband wants it more than my son. Can you talk to him?
Is my child a contender or pretender?
My son watches Tennis Channel all day. Is this helping?
What are my child's chances of going pro?

My daughter continually makes bad choices. She sabotages herself. Is this a stage?
My daughter seems to self-destructs every tournament. Can you help?

Does my child need mental training?
Why does my child play great in practice, horrible in matches!
My daughter lacks confidence, Why?
There's not enough time in the day! Help!
Why should I chart matches?
How would match logs help?
What's a daily focus journal?
My son's words say he wants to be a pro, his actions say something else, is this normal?
I believe my son's perfectionism is interfering with his performance. Can you help?

How do you beat a moonball, pusher?
Those strategy books seem so technical. Can you make it easy?
My daughter struggles with consistency. Got any tricks?
Is my daughter's style of play right for her?
My son is losing to players he used to beat. Can you help?
Is the game of doubles really that important anymore?
How do we assist our son in decreasing his unforced errors?
Are you saying strokes are not important?
The Painter's Analogy

Brain Types and Body Types
Organizing a Quarterly Schedule for Practice Sessions and Tournaments
Develop Your Child's Secondary Strokes

Practice in the Manner in Which Your Expected to Perform
Nurturing All Four Sides of a Complete Player
Develop Your Child's B and C Game Plans
Cultivate Proactive Patterns
Rehearse Closing Out Sets
Between Point Ritual Rehearsals
Follow Your Child's Customized Evaluation Assessment

Arrange a financial budget
Coordinate a realistic schedule
Manage the instructors
Establish expectations
Systemize the details

Organizing Your Child & Your Team
Off Court Training
Match Day Preparation
On Court Physical (Primary & Secondary Strokes)
On Court Emotional (Issues & Solutions)
On Court Mental (Tactical & Strategic)
Ranking Goals: Organizing your Childs Short and Long Term
Goals

FOREWORD

By Legendary Instructor **Vic Braden**

Like some people, some books enter your life and change it forever. This is one of those rare books! This easy reading manual is fun, accurate and entertaining. It moves gracefully from cover to cover, as it exposes the mysteries and provides unique insight to their solutions. Frank is ahead of the field. This tennis parent guide is a one of a kind gem! Frank's inspiration, motivation and humor prove he is the best kind of teacher. A veteran national level coach and seasoned tennis parent.

What Frank shares with the world is no small gift. He sheds light on the darkest secrets of the junior tennis wars. He connects the hidden dots. Most of all, each section acts as a refresher course on how to be a better tennis parent and coach.

I recommend this book to anybody interested in helping their children reach their full potential on and off the court! The Tennis Parents Bible should be required reading for every inspiring athlete, parent and coach.

Vic Braden,

The Vic Braden Tennis College

ACKNOWLDGEMENTS

My deepest gratitude goes to my wife, Linda, who makes me be a better person each and every day. It was her countless hours of design and editing that brought this book to life. To my step daughter, Sarah, who believed me when I repeatedly said, "If you keep on working this hard, you'll be playing the U.S. Open by age 15". ..Guess what...she did!

Thanks to my literary agent Bob Silverstein who has guided me towards the best of both worlds: Self- publishing The Tennis Parent's Bible as an eBook, as well as, securing a traditional book deal with Human Kinetics Publishing - Championship Tennis. I would also like to thank the USPTA and Theresa Thompson (Editor, Tennis View Magazine) for inviting me to share my tennis knowledge with their readers.

A special thank you goes to Craig Tiley (Tennis Australia) for inviting me to speak at Australia's International Coaching Conferences.

Lastly, a heartfelt thank you goes to Vic Braden. He gave me my start in the industry in 1985. His continuous mentoring has played the most significant role in my development as a coach.

PREFACE

When it comes to the development of the millions of junior tennis players, there's been something missing, something overlooked. That is, until now. I'm pleased to introduce *The Tennis Parent's Bible*.

Tennis teaching professionals, academy directors, college coaches and/or high school coaches who have kept current with behavioral sports science will find this book an excellent reference. For tennis industry individuals who have yet to incorporate organizational or behavioral science into their teaching, this book will provide a wealth of new insights into teaching strategies. For parents of beginning recreational players to advanced tournament players, this book will prove an invaluable developmental tennis guide. For those parents currently in the trenches of junior competition this book will help you critique, re-evaluate and direct your child's tennis team.

Regardless of the stage of development, *The Tennis Parent's Bible* will assist you, the tennis parent, in maximizing your child's tennis potential at the quickest rate.

The evolutionary state of tennis demands parents be more involved and informed, due to the ever increasing demands of the game. The competition is bigger, faster and stronger. Around the globe, the competition is training more efficiently. The days of raising a talented athlete while being a passive parent are long gone. The Tennis Parent's Bible is essential reading for those interested in developing confident, self-reliant and accomplished children.

INTRODUCTION

The Tennis Parent's Bible is comprehensive reference "go to" guide for problem solving. This inspirational book contains many different styles of instructional writing including narration, tales of profound wisdom and motivational stories full of deep insight. *The Tennis Parent's Bible* addresses the importance of fundamental stroke production, nutrition, physiology, proper equipment and off-court training, but it is not intended to be a manual for such topics.

The book sections are designed to be read in any order, in many different settings and independently of each other. This stand out, organizational manual is designed to assist parents and coaches through the mental and emotional complexities of raising a world class young adult through the game of tennis. Included are foundation essentials, blunders and cures, common and not so common questions and answers, difficult problems and their solutions.

Also included are educational tennis tools needed to help identify a player's strengths and weakness, such as a sample weekly planner, pop quizzes, match charts, match logs and daily focus journals. Additional insight into the importance of proper mental and emotional training is supported with an inspirational, in-depth interview with ATP star Sam Querrey. As a bonus, a customized 14 page evaluation is included. The book concludes with a list of invaluable tennis resources.

In the past 25 years, I've estimated spending approximately 45,500 hours on court with ranked juniors, fed roughly 32 million tennis balls, missed 5200 family dinners, 526 family weekend events and 189 holidays due to national tennis events. Why? I love what I do and I'm just getting started!

"As important as the coach's role is, the tennis parent's role is tenfold more important."

Nick Bollettieri

"Pro tour players rate their parents as playing the most significant role in their overall development."

Sports Excellence

Most parents spend 100 percent of their time, money and energy on developing their child's fundamental strokes. Yet, in competitive match play, they blame their lack of results on mental and emotional issues. I have never heard a top ranked junior walk off the court and cry "If I only had followed through higher I would have beat that guy!" What we do hear day in and day out is "I can't stand playing pushers!" or "I was hooked out of the match!" or "I was up again 5-2 and choked!" or "I'm sooo bad!"... Sound familiar?

Millions of children enter the game each year. Unfortunately, many talented athletes leave the game due to a lack of proper mental and emotional development. The aim of this book is to provide the deeper insights needed to progress in such a challenging individual sport.

Throughout the chapters, you will notice repetition of some of the most important mental and emotional factors. In my opinion, this is just as important as stroke repetition. It is my intent to hit the reader with these little pearls of wisdom often enough to guarantee that they sink in.

The mission of *The Tennis Parent's Bible* is to produce world class young adults on and off the tennis court.

PART ONE:

HOW TO BE A WORLD CLASS TENNIS PARENT

"Junior tennis champions are born from great sacrifice. They are never the result of selfish parents."

Outstanding parents are outstanding teachers. The parent is the most important adult figure that will define, mold and shape a child. An experienced coach may assist in developing technical tools such as topspin backhands or a slice serve and a trainer may assist in developing core strength. But, please never underestimate the power of your child's greatest teacher…you!

The job description of a tennis parent is to provide a safe and loving environment. A tennis parent nurtures the physical, mental, emotional and spiritual growth of the child.

A gifted athlete with the desire, work ethic and character of a champion will never achieve his or her full potential without the loving support of a tennis parent/manager. It is your job to push them just beyond their current capabilities. The success of your child on and off the tennis court will depend on your support and parental philosophy.

"A junior competitor without an educated tennis parent is like a ship without a rudder."

The following 10 developmental behaviors represent the essential foundation of a world class tennis parent.

1. Nurturing a Plan

Terrific children, wonderful adults and tennis champions aren't born, they are developed. It's not simply heredity. It is an organized plan. No one becomes extraordinary on their own. The Williams sisters are an actual example of a parent with a plan! The story goes; Richard Williams planned to have more children for the sole purpose of developing them into professional tennis players. Wayne Bryan also had a plan with his twin boys, the Bryan brothers. Without an actual plan, you'll never know your child's true capability.

Preparing an organizational blue print will save you thousands of dollars annually. It will also save your child thousands of wasted, unproductive hours, sweat and tears. Applying this book's comprehensive guide will assist you, the tennis parent, in having a world class plan!

Your child is born with a unique genetic predisposition. Your child is pre-wired with a specific brain and body type. Consider it carefully as you and your coaches (your team) nurture your child's talent. This is an important consideration at all levels of the game.

So, what's the key to maximizing success in the shortest period of time? Is it purchase the latest equipment? Maybe it's hiring a great local pro? What if I said neither? The first and most important tool you will ever apply is discovering your child's personality and brain design.

Old school tennis teaching looks a lot like this. The local pro Jose Gonzales came to the United States from Chile. He was a terrific collegiate player earning a full scholarship to Virginia Commonwealth. Jose even played a few ATP pro challenger events. He found success by being extremely patient. He had a natural gift with his quick feet and he enjoyed running. He took delight in being a steady counter puncher. Jose's shot tolerance was a 20-ball rally!

As a teaching professional, he demands that each of his students abide by his playing style, disciplines and logic. Your thinking, boy that guy sounds pretty experienced, let's hire him as our child's coach! So, is this the right mentor for your child?

The answer is, not likely. Why? Because Jose demands that each student plays his style. The style of tennis that your child needs in order to thrive is based on his or hers own unique design. AKA: brain and body type.

Asking your child to play tennis in a style that opposes their skill sets, beliefs and temperament is a recipe for disaster. This is especially true at the beginning levels of player development. One of the quickest ways to ensure that your child will *quit* the sport is to demand that they play a style that opposes their brain and body type.

Understanding brain and body types is one of the first steps to becoming a world class parent. We'll visit my friend Jon Niednagel's brain type assessment more in the blunder section of this guide (Part Three: Nurturing Character Blunders).

2. Developing a Family Philosophy

At the competitive level, being a tennis parent is one of the most incredibly rewarding, yet most challenging adventures you will ever undertake. Parents with a clear understanding of their own family's unique "life's philosophy" are more likely to avoid drama, stress and misunderstandings.

Asking your child to be mentally tough under adverse conditions, if you the parent cannot control your own anxiety, destroys the positive messages you are trying to deliver. Tennis builds character. On a daily basis, I encourage you the parents to display the same positive character traits developed through sports. This is critical in solidifying these powerful life lessons. The family's philosophy is the basic beliefs, attitudes and moral compass of the group. Let's look at a former client and take a peek into his family philosophy.

Medviv Terknova's daughter, Anna was a student of mine for a short while. My coaching and life philosophy didn't quite gel with Medviv's family philosophy.

Medviv Terknova came from Novosibirsk City, Siberia with his 10 year old little girl. He heard about a Russian girl named Maria Sharapova and had been following her endorsement contracts. In 2009, it rose above the $200 million dollar mark.

Medviv's philosophy was simple. He'll do anything to provide for his daughter Anna. Med left his wife Anka and two children, Provic and Zoron back in Siberia in their 600 square foot apartment. He hadn't seen them in over a year.

Medviv changed his daughter Anna's birth date from October 1998 to 2000 on her passport because he wanted to give her an edge in the U.S. tournament rankings. Medviv stood 5 '6'' and wanted his daughter to be taller. So he had his daughter injected with experimental growth hormones to ensure that she reach a competitive height.

Medviv washed dishes and performed menial labor at his daughter's academy in exchange for tuition. Medviv was a dictator-style parent and could be heard at every practice session screaming advice through the chain link fence. In Anna's matches, Medviv would often applaud the opponent's errors and quietly smirk as Anna cheated at the right times. His philosophy is that "nothing will stand in my way."

Is this family philosophy right for you? I hope not! It may be tempting for some to employ unethical tactics at the lower levels of competition to gain an advantage, but those tactics are unavailable at the higher levels. National finals, college tennis and pro tour tennis have linesman and umpires. Cheating only creates a false sense of security. Those who have relied on manipulating, cheating and gamesmanship as their primary weapon in junior tennis match play lack the essential self-confidence needed at higher level tennis.

Developing your own philosophy will help you, your spouse and children to avoid unnecessary pressure, strain and tension. Having pre-set guidelines will assist you in the development of your child's personal philosophy. It will also aid you in acquiring the right coaches through the different stages of your child's development.

3. Choosing a Parental Style

It's in your best interest to gain an understanding about the parental styles of both you and your spouse. The team leader, who is the primary tennis parent, must cultivate a positive family atmosphere to maximize success. An important step is to define the roles and style of the parent. So what is your primary style?

If you are not sure, or if your ego won't allow you to be pigeon holed, ask your child! They'll laugh as they spot exactly who you are! Here are ten parental styles we see weekly:

The Rocket Scientist: These parents often talk above their child's head, confusing their child more than they help him.

The Athlete: These parents still views them-selves as a competitive athlete. They often stretch more before their child's match than their child does!

The Submissive Victim: She just stands there and takes it as her daughter says, "My mom is so stupid! She doesn't know anything! She doesn't even play!"

The Developer: This parent is always pointing out life lessons in an annoyingly, positive way.

The Drill Sergeant: This parent makes all the decisions in dictator fashion. His battle cry is "Because I said so!"

The Judger: Judging and criticizing is what this parent does best and most often. This parental style can spot 47 things wrong in 30 seconds and they believe they are helping.

The X Pro: "When I was top ranked…" is how most comments start with this parent.

The Negatron: This parental "worrywart" expects the worst in every possible situation.

The Jabber Jaw: Jabber Jaws talk "at" the coach for 45 minutes of the child's 1 hour lesson and then later complains that there wasn't any real progress!

Houdini: This parental type is known to drop off their child at 10am for their 3pm lesson and shows up at the club at 9:30pm to pick them up.

FUN FACT: Children will flourish or shut down depending on the parental style chosen. The best teachers and parents understand that it is our job to get into their world. It is not the child's job to be forced into ours! Respect their personality type.

4. Cultivating Life Lessons

Choosing to embark on this journey has lifelong benefits. It is widely known that having your child participate in the game of tennis is cultivating life lessons. Tennis is an individual, elite sport. Participation in the game of tennis breeds leaders. Congratulations for developing leadership qualities in your child.

The game of tennis teaches the ability to understand and develop the following traits:

1) Time management

2) Adaptability and flexibility skills

3) Ability to handle adversity

4) Ability to handle stress

5) Courage

6) A positive work ethic

7) Perseverance

8) Setting priorities

9) Goal setting

10) Sticking to commitments

11) Determination

12) Problem solving skills

13) Spotting patterns and tendencies

14) Discipline

15) The understanding of fair play and sportsmanship

16) The development of focus

17) Persistence

18) The importance of preparation

19) Dedication and self-control

20) Positive self-image

My favorite life lesson of the top 20 is persistence. As a coach, to see a talented player without persistence or the willingness to sacrifice and work hard is my worst nightmare! That is why at every level it is often the less talented who are willing to pay the price with smart work, and they have all the trophies!

"Nothing is more common than unsuccessful tennis players with tons of physical talent."

Finding a way through a tough opponent even though you're having a bad day is persistence. Staying in the right side of your brain even when things are clearly not going well is persistence. Staying engaged until the very last point is persistence. Now you know my favorite life lesson. What's yours?

5. Understanding the Parental Objective

I asked several clients with juniors of all levels why they chose tennis as their child's primary sport. I found the reasons hilarious yet interesting.

<u>Here are the Parental Responses:</u>

- "Recreational activity, to have fun and get in shape

- "Family bonding"

- "To develop athletic skills"

- "To amplify my son's competitive nature"

- "Because Kelly would look darling in a little tennis dress"

- "I needed a hobby for my wife"

- "To give my child the opportunity that I never had"

- "To one-up my brother- in- law and his all- star kid"

- "To help them get into a great college"

- "My son tried the real sports, you know football and basketball. He wasn't so good, so we're down to tennis"

- "To enjoy the sport I love"

- "I want my son to experience playing a high school varsity sport"

- "To be with like-minded people"

- "To keep my daughter active and busy throughout her teenage years, so she's less likely to get into trouble"

- "To attract a full college scholarship"

- "My goal is to have my daughter playing on the WTA pro tour by the age of 17"

- "I wanted my son to be involved in the sport that gave me so much."

- "To one up my neighbors…power baby!"

So, how important are these issues to you? What are your reasons for pursuing the sport? Have you considered your child's reasons?

6. Identifying the Levels of Competitive Tennis

Recreational tennis is enjoyed by millions of junior players in the United States. The emphasis is on exercise, fundamental athletic skills, tons of fun, wearing the outfits, participation by all, and social interactions. As skills are developed the recreational and social game is replaced by a new game called competitive tennis.

Different United States Tennis Association (USTA) sections proudly offer their unique versions of junior social competition in the forms of junior leagues, club junior teams and high school junior varsity levels. As players progress, they graduate to sectional competition in the forms of satellite tournaments, novice tournaments, open level tournaments, high school varsity, invitational or designated events. Players reaching the higher levels of their sectional events graduate to the national 1, 2, 3 level events. Teens peaking at the top of the national level shift their focus to the International Tennis Federation (ITF) world rankings.

At the age of 15, competitive juniors begin to shift their focus toward college tennis. On rare occasions, the world's best youngsters begin to try their luck at the minor league levels of the professional game. Females from the age of 14 and boys from the age of 17 are found testing their skills on the Futures and Challenger tours, Association of Tennis Professionals (ATP), Women's Tennis Association (WTA) main professional tours.

Juniors winning national titles or establishing a high ITF ranking earn the right to be offered the elusive wild card entries into U.S. Pro events by the USTA.

"You will win games when you focus one point at a time....

You will win sets when you focus one game at a time....

You will win matches when you focus one set at a time....

You will win tournaments when you focus one match at a time"

Frank Giampaolo

There are seldom shortcuts to success. Later, in the tennis parent blunder chapter, we'll be discussing, in detail, when to move up to the next level of competition.

7. Considering the Economics of Tennis

The economics vary from level-to-level and city-to-city, taking account the families established living expectations. Recreational tennis at a city park is basically free! The beauty of the sport is that it is accessible to everyone! Competitive tennis is a different animal. If you're reading this book, my bet is that your child has progressed nicely into the competitive levels. As we peak into the economics of the game, it's important to keep in mind that only by risking going too far, can you find out how far your child can go.

Let's take a look at the extreme! Chasing big dreams comes with a big price tag! To illustrate this point, here is an actual client of mine. This young man is 16 years old with a USTA national ranking in the top 30. He works hard on his game an average of 20 hours a week. He is committed and works his tail off.

Here is an estimation of his actual tennis related expenses. The bottom line is that it breaks down to roughly $96.07 a day or $34,640.00 annually. A quarterly expense report for this typical top nationally ranked junior in Southern California looks like the following:

Estimated Quarterly (Every 3 month) Expense Report:

Driving to & from tennis: $720.00
Meals on the road: $1,200.00
Tennis academies or clinics: $1,440.00
Off-court training: $1,200.00
Tennis lessons: $2,400.00
Equipment strings and grips only: $600.00
Clothes 3 outfits / 1 pair of tennis shoes: $350.00
Tournament registration: $450.00
Two nights in a hotel: $300.00

Quarterly Estimated Total: $8,660.00

Fundraising

A few ways to help with the costs of chasing the dream are:

1) Solicit family and friends as sponsors

2) Seek out business or corporate sponsorships in exchange for positive press in the local paper.

3) Make a Facebook page and personal website. Include a PayPal "Donate" button. Post the travel schedule, achievements, rankings and results.

4) Fundraising events at the local club. Encourage product donations to be raffled off. Seek out local celebrities and/or teaching professionals to participate in a social mixed doubles event. Charge a fee for members and guests to participate. Advertise in the local newspaper, at surrounding tennis clubs and through the internet.

Estimated Annual Expenses of National Level Sports

The bottom line is that to develop any world class level athlete takes serious money. Be grateful, it could be worse. Here is an example of estimated costs (found on Google) of individual national level sports and their estimated average annual price tag:

- Cycling and Paintball - $18,000 - $40,000

- Dance and Cheer - $50,000 - $70,000

- Golf and Tennis - $40,000 – $80,000

- Gymnastics and Figure Skating - $70,000 – $100,000

- Equestrian, Yachting and Motocross - $80,000 – $150,000

    And you thought you had it bad ☺

8. Establishing Expectations and Guidelines

Since you are still in shock from the above expense report, this may be a wonderful time to assist you in organizing your expectation speech! Parents have to communicate their expectations to their child during both practice as well as match play. This is especially important in the beginner and intermediate levels of the game.

It may also be in your best interest to share these with your child's primary coach. You will develop an alliance by clarifying your expectations and guidelines. When speaking with your child, avoid starting with the standard "When I was your age, I had to walk to school uphill…in the snow…both ways…"

Here are my top twenty practice session tennis parental expectations:

1) Place the improvement of your performance over having to win the match, social game or live ball drill.

2) On the court be grateful, enthusiastic and polite.

3) Arrive 10 minutes before your scheduled practice session to stretch.

4) Arrive on court dressed and ready to compete.

5) Avoid complaining or criticizing others.

6) Give the coach your best efforts and your undivided attention.

7) When the coach is talking, hold the balls. Stop, look him/her in the eyes and listen.

8) No cell phones allowed on court.

9) Move quickly between drills and during ball pick up – yes, the student helps pick up balls!

10) Hustle and give 100% effort.

11) Avoid negative tones, body language and facial expressions.

12) Avoid using profanity.

13) Admit mistakes and understand the cause of the error.

14) Come to practice with a pre-set game plan and an eagerness to learn.

15) Be open to constructive criticism.

16) Be willing to develop your weaknesses.

17) Stay fully committed and focused for the entire training session.

18) Rehearse staying in a positive frame of mind for the entire training session.

19) Take full responsibility for your words and actions.

20) Practice in the manner you are expected to perform.

Ask your child to challenge themselves daily. Remind them that choosing to train below their capability breeds "mediocrity."

9. Listening

(Written by a teenage girl to her father)

Dear Dad,

What I'm about to say is hard for me. So hard I can't seem to look you in the eyes and say what I want to say. I guess I'm afraid.

Maybe it's best this way. Maybe you'll listen with your eyes since you haven't been hearing me. Maybe you just want to see what you want to see. That's the champion you've been forcing me to be.

Dad, are you listening?

I know you want what's best for me. I know you believe all the messages you're sending will make me a better player. Dad, communication isn't just sending messages, it's also receiving them.

Dad, are you listening?

Look at my face, there is no joy. I'm angry all the time. I still continue to play week

after week, tournament after tournament.
I'm sad. No I'm miserable. Why can't you
see that? Do you notice any of this?

I utter how I hate competing. I protest every
single practice and yet you push me to try
harder. You demand, "Be tougher Sasha,
you have to aim to be perfect!" Well Dad,
I'm not perfect. I just want to be normal.

Dad, are you listening?

I'm depressed and confused and feel that
this life is your life, not mine! I love you. I
don't want to hurt you. I'm sorry. Please
forgive me but I don't think I want to play
tennis any more.

Dad, are you listening?

Love, Sasha

On the other side of this coin, is whether gently pushing your child through a difficult stage in their career/development is the right thing to do? You bet! There isn't a single champion who didn't have a parent or paid authority figure pushing them past their comfort zone or carrying them when they couldn't go on. After he received the letter, I met with Sasha's Dad and my advice was this:

Stan ask Sasha this question, "Would it be alright to take a one month sabbatical?" Then, take her rackets away and hide them. Don't even mention the word tennis to her. If she never again brings up the subject, then she is done. That means you have a normal, healthy, average child. Go on vacations, enjoy weekends and appreciate your family!

If the game begins to pull her back, then she'll be engaged for all the right reasons. It's about choices. Giving her some time to see for herself that being an average teen, playing video games, texting nonsense to her friends and hanging out at the same mall every weekend isn't all that it's cracked up to be. She needs to see for herself that the grass isn't always greener. She's a great kid. She's got talent. Trust me, just let this play out.

NOTE: By the tenth night of Sasha's sabbatical, she was bored to tears. She came into her parent's room and asked if they can hit a few balls tomorrow. Sasha went on a tear. She has won two national titles in the just last months.

10. Mandatory Monthly Video & Pizza Nights Meetings

I can assure you, at every level, the parent/player relationship will be emotionally demanding. Although tennis is an individual sport, it takes a supportive team to excel at the competitive level. Leading the team, the parent will often take the "brunt" of the player's frustrations. As a result, the parent/player relationship will take time, patience, effort, thought, love and creativity.

A preventative measure to avoiding much of the drama of this demanding sport is organizing a monthly mandatory family meeting. You may be saying, "What is he talking about, we are always together. What good would family night do?"

Family night should provide a positive, non-threatening atmosphere in which you can talk about the direction of your child's training. Often we are so deep in the trenches that we lose the larger picture of our path or direction. The monthly meeting will bring clarity to your organization.

The evening begins with a simple casual meal and a relaxed discussion. The most critical component to this evening is you, the parent, taking the time to LISTEN to your child. The evening will end with a video of one of your child's recent matches to be reviewed and analyzed. The number one learning style is the visual learner. Trust me, seeing is believing!

While viewing the match, ask your child to spot tendencies, chart unforced errors to winners, spot offense, neutral and defensive opportunities...etc. Set a time limitation for viewing the video. Remember this is supposed to be a positive communication exchange.

Dinner Time Topics May Include:

1) Academics

2) Family relationships/roles

3) Social relationships

4) Relaxing and down time scheduling

5) Periodizational training schedule

6) Tournament scheduling

7) Equipment issues

8) Coaches, trainer, hitter issues

9) Match play emotions

10) Match play strategies, tactics and shot selections

11) Current injuries and injury prevention

12) Nutrition and hydration issues

13) Playing in the current elements

14) Visualization rituals

15) Primary or secondary stroke issues

16) Accountability and attitude

17) Handling gamesmanship

18) Spotting burn out

19) Common traits of athletic champions

20) Current challenges

A large part of these monthly team meetings is to nurture your child's ability to care. They have to care about themselves first and foremost. If they truly care about their dreams and goals it's amazing what they can accomplish.

"You can achieve it…only if you believe it."

On the other side, they also need to be reminded to care about their family, friends, coaches and trainers. Fostering empathy and concern towards others builds their positive character. Multiplying and digesting positive character is critical because stressful competition reveals what is on the inside. That is one's true character.

PART TWO:

UNDERSTANDING TALENT

What is Talent?

Talent is considered by most to be a genetic predisposition, a sense of natural ability handed down through the family gene pool. Expert educators in various fields agree that every decade one truly gifted individual walks through their door. Does this mean that most truly successful people aren't genuinely talented or does it mean that talent is more than merely good genes?

Talent is really a foreshadowing of future greatness. It's a kid with potential. No, it's even more than that. It's a kid with potential with parents who were deeply involved in the development of skills and the stimulation of passion.

So, what does this new definition of talent mean for the rest of us mere mortals? It means that if a child has parents who are determined and passionate about the game and extremely persistent, they've got a real shot at greatness!

In every field talent is a learned behavior. What do Wayne Gretsky, Yo-Yo Ma, Bill Gates, Bobby Fischer, Tiger Woods, Mozart and Michelangelo have in common with tennis greats? They were all children who developed a remarkable talent from an early age. A spark was lit, they grew passion and the spark became a flame as they persistently developed talent. What seems like a god given natural gift is actually a learned behavior.

FUN FACT: Talent is determination, passion and persistence. In junior competition, why do youngsters with a natural flair for strokes lose to seemingly less talented players? Naturally athletic children are able to acquire the physical skills of the game so effortlessly that they often don't apply themselves to train the mandatory mental and emotional components of winning tennis. What matters the most is drive, persistence and work ethic.

How to Stimulate Your Young Talent?

In my opinion, most of the ATP and WTA professionals you watch on television did not demonstrate early phenomenal promise. They simply were solid athletes, with potential who were nurtured the love for the game twenty hours a week.

The best players were motivated by very powerful forces. Find out what is motivating your child?

Common motivational forces vary from:

1) Having to keep up with older siblings

2) Ensure a better future

3) Seeing someone just like them succeed

4) An experienced coach who believes in them

5) Wanting to belong

6) Deep need for a better life

7) Fame

8) Fortune

9) Supportive parents

10) Love for the game

FUN FACT: The Russian tennis revolution was motivated by poverty as well as seeing a compatriot named Anna Kournikova break through and become rich and famous.

Talent is passion and persistence, right? It doesn't matter where you're from. It doesn't even matter how much money you have, or which God you pray to, or if you're a member of the country club. Talent isn't dependent on whether or not your child is wearing their lucky shorts! Talent is about dedication, tenacity and hard work.

SPECIAL NOTE: When Andy Roddick is home in Austin, TX. He does his off-court training on the local high schools track and hits tennis balls at the park up the street from his house!

How is Talent Measured?

Talent is most often viewed by the champs past success. We all know Roger Federer is talented. Why? Because he wins! We see his confidence radiating as we watch his fluid strokes and graceful movement on the court. But what predetermined his success? What enticed him? What factors built his passion? How did he develop persistence?

Let's use my step- daughter Sarah Fansler as a quantifiable example of gauging the development of a kid's potential. Most would agree that Sarah has a flair for the game. She was ranked top in the nation. Sarah won multiple gold, silver and bronze balls. She won a total of 10 U.S. national titles. She's played the junior U.S. Open twice and the adult U.S. Open once before the age of 16. She was honored as he NCAA College Freshman of the year at USC.

Now, let's uncover her underlying story and take a deeper look at Sarah's training regimen. As a junior player, Sarah had spent six years training full time. That's about 20 hours a week, or a thousand hours a year practicing in the manner in which she is expected to perform.

Sarah did a private lesson with me from 6:30am -7:30am before getting ready for school. Sarah's after-school regime included sparring with a college player, playing full practice matches and/or off-court training at a specialized gym called "Get Fit", a Vert system off-court training center. After dinner Sarah and I drilled for an additional hour and a half. On weekends, Sarah played tournaments.

Sarah followed this books formula of deep accelerated learning. Her training regimen was more intense than the typical training program of a high performance player. The hidden factor to her tennis success was her hard work on and off the court each week. The accelerated learning process catapulted Sarah above her rivals.

So, was Sarah's success due to her natural gifts or was it earned through a planned process? My answer is that 20 percent of Sarah's junior success was due to her natural talents, 80 percent was due to her learned behaviors.

How Do We Manage Talent?

It's our job as tennis parents to organize accelerated learning. Accelerated learning is tapping into your child's genetic predisposition and then nurturing the best possible style of play. A marvelous example of accelerated learning is skill-set rehearsals. Progressing a talented athlete into the higher levels of competition is done by shifting focus back and forth from consistent- skill sets to flexible- skill sets.

What does that mean? Core mechanics (basic strokes) are trained in a controlled environment. These are motor programming sequences that need to be followed. For instance, the hitting zone of every world class stroke follows the same physical laws. This is a consistent- skill set.

On the other side, playing sports like basketball, hockey, soccer or tennis are random multi-changing split second acts. It's about adaptation, creativity, spotting options and aborting missions. Flexibility and millisecond decision making on the fly is a critical function of these types of sports. This is what we call flexible-skill sets.

SPECIAL NOTE: Learning how to stroke a ball and learning how to win tournaments require learning the two different skill sets and brain functions. What's best for your child, at this stage in their development depends on numerous factors. Use the customized evaluation chapter to personalize your child's training regimen.

FUN FACT: Different sports require different brain functions and development. A world class figure skater or gymnast simply focuses on recreating the correct sequence. Their performance goal is to match their exact pre- determined routine. In their performance they only recreate, they don't create. So, would they train with flexible-skill sets? Not likely. Should a tennis player? You bet!

Managing the talent is promoting, inspiring and encouraging both stationary development and live ball random sessions.

Nurture your youngster to be a complete player by focusing on all four sides of development:

1.) Primary and secondary stroke production skills

2.) Shot and pattern selection skills

3.) Movement and fitness skills

4.) Focus and emotional control skills

Developing all four sides at an early age will increase the learning speed tenfold. It doesn't matter if your child simply wants to make the local high school junior varsity squad or if your child has a long term goal of playing on the pro tour, understanding and applying this books success formula is critical.

Remember, from the parent's side, skill building is really consistent confidence building. Regardless of your child's career path, success is a result of passionate and persistent guidance.

PART THREE:

THE TOP 50
TENNIS PARENT BLUNDERS
& HOW TO AVOID THEM

NURTURING CHARACTER BLUNDERS

Ignoring Your Child's Brain and Body Type

I mentioned this blunder earlier. Your child has a genetic predisposition to excel at a particular style of tennis. A common parental mistake is assuming that your child is wired like you! Most likely they have a different brain type. They may see the world differently and approach tasks differently than you would.

I've found that by understanding each player's brain type, body type and personality traits; there are similar obstacles and skills. Similar frustration tolerance levels, similar styles of play and decision making abilities.

The player's upbringing, family, friends, and cultural environment also play a large part in shaping their game. This is called the "nurture" side. The two sides are nature and nurture.

To dig deeper into brain typing I suggest you visit my friend John Niednagel's site: www.braintypes.com . I suggest, that you first take a few minutes to accurately brain type yourself, your spouse and each family member. It may open a whole new world of communication!

FUN FACT: Dozens of my students annually win their first National title and skyrocket their rankings by applying brain typing. My students, Arthur Karagezian jumped from the mid 700's nationally to top 30 nationally, Gannon Daynes jumped from the mid 500's nationally to top 50 nationally. Their training was systematically customized to their unique brain and body types and their rankings greatly improved.

Managing Without Guidance

Would you expect a talented, beginner athlete to be a world champion without proper coaching? Not likely. As a parent, plan on seeking out assistance and guidance through this journey. In today's world, coaching has moved past the athletic playing fields and into every aspect of life. One of the best kept secrets of the successful junior tennis champion is a knowledgeable, educated primary tennis parent.

Parental coaching can be done in-person, by phone, in groups or in private, customized settings. Wonderful skills can be developed through attending seminars, Googling topics of interest, watching the Tennis Channel, accompanying your youngster to college or professional matches or purchasing instructional DVD's and books!

Serena Williams said her parents learned how to coach her by watching Vic Braden instructional videos. Seek out those who can help you make clearer decisions for your child and your family. Like gasoline and fire, your education can accelerate your child's success!

Being an Unaccountable Parent

Let's look briefly at a typical open ranked junior player's schedule:

There's 168 hours in a week. Sleeping takes up roughly 56 hours, school/homework takes up roughly 60 hours, high performance tennis training takes up 15-20 hours, add on travel and meals, and the average player is still left with approximately 25 hours unaccounted for. Unaccountable players believe they don't have enough time to train. Organized and accountable players know there is plenty of time to train!

Another side of accountability is based on the fact that national tournaments are often held over holiday breaks. Do you choose to spend Thanksgiving at home with your family and friends or are you okay spending Thanksgiving in a hotel out of state? Here's another interesting accountability issue: Do you choose to remain home so your child can prepare properly for the winter nationals or do you choose to go skiing the week before the event? "You can't have your cake and eat it too!"

Underestimating the Success Formula

Here it is folks. It is called the 10,000 hour rule. For approximately ten years; your child should be spending 20 hours per week in tennis related activities to become a world-class player. (The 10,000 hour rule applies to all fields of expertise)

SPECIAL NOTE: Quality is more important than quantity. My daughter went from a 10 years old beginner to playing the U.S. Open in 6 years or 6,000 hours. How? By practicing in the manner she's expected to perform versus simply hitting balls.

Chapter three outlines a weekly organizational plan to plan for success. Use this to customize your youngsters blue print for success.

FUN FACT: The 10 year rule was first applied as far back as 1899.

Avoiding the Nurturing Component

Guess who was an angry emotional train wreck as a junior competitor? If you said Andre Agassi, Rafael Nadal, Roger Federer and even the iceman Bjorn Borg, then you're right! Moral excellence is a maturing process. Everyone can compete in a relaxed, happy state, but not everyone wants to. Let's cover that again. Everyone can compete in a relaxed, happy state, but not everyone wants to!

Often negative behavior has been motor programmed into the player's routine. It is a comfortable, dirty, old habit. The development of character lies in the ability to first learn to be uncomfortable competing without the negative act. It's like a stand-up comedian without his props to hide behind. The old props are comfortable.

The insight lies in the understanding that each player has a character choice. Somewhere in their late teens; Borg, Federer and Nadal *were* taught a wiser code of conduct and chose to apply it.

Encouraging Dependency

A serious blunder is "selling "dependence. I've seen numerous parents and teaching pros fall into this category. Often parents and coaches live vicariously through their super stars. Their fear of being abandoned by the champ motivates them to develop a dependency. We often hear the player's position as they communicate their feelings during their 20-page evaluation session. The players live in fear because a parent or coach has insinuated "I'm the only one who can save you" or "I don't ever want to catch you hitting with another pro because they'll mess up your game!"

Successful national champions have developed the physical, mental and emotional tools to solve their own problems. It's our job to assist them in solving their own problems!

Here's what I did as a tennis parent from the time my step daughter was 12 years old attending her first national event.

"Ok Sarah, this is your event. I'm here to assist you every step of the way. Let's play the co-pilot game. Sarah, I can't drive and read the map. Can you please find the way to the airport? Great! Now find the parking structure. What's our airline? Read the signs and lead the way. Terrific!

As we de-planed, I would ask Sarah, "Can you follow the signs to baggage claim?" That was easy. Now, were searching for Alamo rental cars, I wonder what kind of car is in slot #26? What's your guess? Oh no... a P.T. Cruiser...Not again!!! "Sarah, can you read the map and direct us to the hotel?"

Lastly, were going to hit for a half hour tonight on the tournament courts so you can sleep easy knowing the surroundings. "Can you co-pilot us to the tournament site?"

Was it easy, nope. It was like pulling teeth! It would have been a hundred times faster and easier if I had made her dependent on me. Did she learn self-reliance? Did she develop confidence in her abilities with the unknown? Did she become an independent thinker? You bet! By the age of 15, Sarah was flying comfortably, without us, around the country, as well as in England, Germany and Australia to compete.

Talking Economics Before/After a Match

Dumping unnecessary loads of pressure on a player before or after a match is one of the most common mistakes. I have often heard parents say "If you lose one more time to someone ranked lower than you, we're pulling the plug! Do you know how much we spend on your tennis?"

How do you expect them to hit their performance goals, if you are stressing them out about finances?

FYI: An average family with a young tournament player participating in local/ sectional events spends an average of $300.00-$500.00 per week on tennis related activities!

Thinking Perfect Strokes are Mandatory

Legendary star Andre Agassi states in his book that he was still learning how to volley when he retired. Pete Sampras wasn't thrilled with his topspin backhand. John McEnroe is quoted as saying "Nobody has perfect strokes; it's what you do with what you've got that counts!" They simply competed with their secret weaknesses. Learn how to expose your strengths and hide your weaknesses!

Parents, players and coaches who are waiting for every stroke to be perfect before they begin to compete are missing the boat. Every national champion I've ever coached had holes in their game as they held up the gold ball. The trick is learning how to compete with imperfections.

Even if your child did possess perfect strokes on the practice court, different strokes will occasionally break down at different stages of an event. Dealing with imperfection with back up plans are a tools in your child's tool belt.

Managing Without a "Hollywood" Script

Hollywood parents with "wanna be" child stars have the reputation for being a little nuts right? Hollywood parents drag their kids from audition to audition in search of ways to live vicariously through their kids. Well...I don't recommend that. What I do recommend is asking your child to use the system that Hollywood stars use when working on a sit com. Here's their four part system:

1) First, they get the script for a show (Your child gets a script for how to beat a moonballer. Yes, don't worry the script is in here).

2) Second, the Hollywood star spends hours running the lines (Your child will ask a hitting coach to run the patterns used to beat those pesky pushers).

3) Third, the Hollywood stars spend the week doing dress rehearsals (Your child has to run those patterns on the practice court, in practice sets often for weeks at a time doing dress rehearsals).

4) Fourth, the actors shoot the show in front of a live audience (Your child plays the actual tournament). All too often our junior competitors learn a wonderful pattern, and then they choose not to rehearse the patterns on the practice court. They choose to forget about actually doing any dress rehearsals and wonder why they lose to another moonballer!

Parents, use this four part method to develop your child's game: Learn it, Memorize it, Rehearse it and Achieve it.

Ignoring Off-Court Training, Proper Nutrition and Hydration

What does off court training have to do with the mental side? When the player gets fatigued their movement gets sloppy, their stroke spacing is off and unforced errors begin to fly off their racket. Poor decision making and negative emotions set in. Often, the actual cause of a child's emotional breakdown is lack of fitness. Unfit players do not perform their rituals, they do not spot tendencies and they do not manage their mistake. Poor physical fitness manifests in mental and emotional breakdowns. For instance, most juniors go for low percentage shots due to the fact that they are too tired to grind out the point. So is off-court training linked to the mental side? Absolutely!

Proper hydration and nutrition is also a critical factor in the physical, mental and emotional links of every tennis competitor. As parents, we have to insist that our players fuel up before battle. Dehydration triggers fatigue, dizziness, headaches and nausea. Improper nutrition lowers the blood sugar levels to the brain. Improper nutrition and hydration guarantees poor decision making skills at crunch time.

MAINTAINING POSITIVE COMMUNICATION BLUNDERS

"Good judgment comes from experience. Experience comes from bad judgment."

Not Acknowledging Your Child's Efforts

Once a month, throughout the course of your youngsters tennis career plan on sitting down and writing a letter stating how proud you are of them. Place it on their bed at night.

Parents, do you realize that most full grown adults don't focus on their job 100 percent of the time! They may be at work, but what are they actually doing? It's my bet that most adults could not handle the pressure a serious junior competitor endures day in and day out. Take a few moments to acknowledge how proud you are of their efforts. Thank them for the courage they show as they lay it on the line week after week.

Asking your Child to Fix a Flawed Stroke While Keeping Them on the Tournament Trail

It takes about four- to -six weeks for a new motor program to override an old one. The success rate of actually fixing a flawed stroke fluctuates. It depends greatly on the talent, work ethic; professional advice and allotted time spend deprogramming the old stroke while re-wiring the new motor program.

The actual progression works like this. You decide it's best to fix a flawed stroke. So, on week one your child has 90 percent of the old motor program (doing it the old way) and only 10 percent of the new motor program (when they actually feel the new program correctly). During week two, the progression slides from still around 70 percent old motor program to 30% new. At three weeks into the new development, your child will perform about 50/50. Now the fun begins! Week four, the new motor program starts to override the old one at only 40 percent old to 60 percent new! By week five, it's at 30 percent old to 70 percent new. By week six, the old motor program is almost eliminated. It shows up about 10 percent of the time as the new improved stroke is programmed to replace it.

Issues arise when you put your child into a competitive situation without giving the new motor program the time it takes to override the old one.

If you put your child into a competitive situation before the six-week replacement phase is complete, you are absolutely guaranteeing that your child will go back to the old, but flawed "comfortable" stroke. Now guess who just wasted all that money on the lessons to correct the flaw? You!

Playing Them Up Too Soon

In Part One, we discussed the different levels of junior competition. A player should prove themselves in a certain level of competition before jumping to the higher level. I recommend that a child win two events in a division before you bump them up to a higher age division. It's a bad idea to bump them up because they can't handle playing their peers. This applies to practice sets as well! Players need to rehearse closing out matches against different styles and levels of players.

Talking at Visual Learners

Mr. Kolouski says to me, "I've explained numerous times to my son, about decreasing the racket face angle 30 degrees. I told him to rotate his right palm a quarter of a turn. I've expounded on the 60 degree lift through the shoulder hinge. I decipher things for hours. I explain everything in detail, yet my son's still confused. I feel like I am conversing with a granite wall!"

Different people have different learning styles or preferences. Getting into your child's world and understanding how he's wired is the key. Remember that a parental and coaching blunder is forcing him to enter your world!

The three preferred learning styles are visual learners, auditory learners and kinesthetic learners. Explaining detail after detail for hours on end to a visual learner is just plain preposterous!

Parents Words That Don't Match Their Actions

Loving parents with great intentions often sabotage their words of wisdom by saying one thing and doing the other. Asking them to be prepared, timely and organized when you're not sends mixed messages. Understand that if rules and laws don't apply to you, don't expect rules and laws to apply to them!

Teaching them not to lie and then lying to your mother- in- law about why you can't make the family Thanksgiving in Cleveland is sending mixed messages. (Ok, I wouldn't necessarily want to spend Thanksgiving in Cleveland either, so you can lie about that one, but not in front of your child).

Ignoring your Non-Verbal Communication

In Malcolm Gladwell's book "Blink", he shares an interesting insight regarding surgeons who make a medical mistake. The bottom line is surgeons with top credentials, but poor bed side manners are more likely to get sued, then are surgeons with the same credentials, making the same mistake, but with terrific bed side manners (Of, course there are exceptions).

A parent or coach with a condescending tone of voice, a disgusted facial expression or even negative body language, is often the trigger that sets your child into a defensive position. Studies show that up to 70 percent of communication is non verbal.

We initially believe that we are helping our children by spotting every single problem and bringing it to light. This "tough love" isn't in their best interest. Instead parents, if you want dynamic results, along with a happier child try adding positive power words to your tennis talks. They include: Great attitude; You're so brave; Terrific energy, You're playing fearless; It's so fun watching you perform; You have guts; You motivate me; You look strong out there; I'm so proud!

After all, isn't that what you wanted to hear from your folks? Every child needs to hear these positive statements from their parents.

Being Arrogant To Lower Ranked Players and Their Parents

Remember the wall the top players had when your child was the newbie? Remember how you felt with the other parents looked right through you?

I challenge you not to make the same mistake they've made! Open your hearts and welcome them. There is a parallel of our attitude towards strangers and our overall happiness. You never know, that new kid just may be your child's doubles partner in a year or two. That new parent may know of a great trainer, coach or academy in the area or information regarding a new tournament. Trust me. The more you give and help others; the more you get back in return.

Criticizing Other Players

I must say, Mom's who've never competed in sports are the worst. Come on, you know who you are! You criticize others in hopes to make you feel bigger. Yet, it leaved you ashamed and deflated.

In my opinion, actions speak louder than words. So, what kind of message are you actually sending your child? Is teaching your child that their parent is actually an ugly person the message you want to send? Look for the positive. Say something nice. If you can't find a single nice thing to say, don't say anything at all!

Talking about Your Child's Peers

At tournament sites we often hear parents and inexperienced coaches unknowingly sabotaging their player's upcoming performance by pulling their attention completely away from their performance goals. They do this by talking about the success of their child's peers.

It's best not to discuss other players lucky draws, their great wins, who's seeded where, other players improved rankings, the past success of the opponent, match outcomes and future ranking speculations. These conversations clutter the players mind with needless distractions and unwanted stress.

NAVIGATING TOURNAMENTS BLUNDERS

"Often you have to lose a few battles to win the war."

Being In- Flexible

One of the most important elements of being a tennis parent lies in your flexibility!

Here are a few examples:

1) You want your child to be invited into a better clinic but it is filled. Three days later the pro calls and says, "There's a slot open…"

2) Then, your child has entered into a local tournament and the start time says 10:00am, you arrive at 9:40am and the tournament director says, "We're backed up, looks like 11: 30am or 12:00pm"

3) A few years later, your child is on an alternate list for a national tournament. Two days before the event, you check the computer and he is in the main draw. Now you have to book your flight and fly to the event by tomorrow.

4) A few months down the road, your daughter wins a super national tournament and the USTA is calling few days before a pro tournament in Florida asking you if you want a wild card. You both fly there, prepared for the week and she loses first round so you fly home that night!

5) Your son's in a $25K pro challenger in Pittsburg. Suddenly 3 ATP players back out of the $100K in Hawaii. Guess what, you'll have to get comfortable being flexible and have a terrific travel agent.

Under Valuating the Importance of Life Skills

Your child needs to develop stroke skills and life skills. Both sets of skills are necessary to progress comfortably through the junior tennis wars.

Chris Langan is best known as the "smartest" man in the United States. My bet is that you've never heard of him and you never will. His IQ is off the charts, but you won't find him impacting the world. Why? It's because he is so inept and frustrated with his inability to deal with people, he lives a very isolated existence. Is it Chris's fault? Yes and no. He wasn't taught social skills as a child. Getting along with people is a tool used to navigate the world. Begin early building your child's navigational tools on and off the court.

Start to build relationships with players, families, stringers and tournament directors. Ask your child to write thank you notes to tournament directors after the event. Make friends with the USTA linesmen. You'll be seeing them year in and year out throughout your child's junior career.

Neglecting Pre-Match Routines

Once your child begins to compete in novice events, players should begin to prepare their own equipment. This is developing organizational skills such as time management and accountability.

Train them to begin preparing equipment a few days before an event. This includes stringing and re-gripping rackets and making sure their lucky shorts are in the laundry getting washed!

The night before the event, assist them in packing their racket bags with rackets, towel, grips, extra shoes, shoe laces, a medical kit, water, Gatorade, power bars or fruit, extra socks and shirts, hat or visors, sun block and their tennis bag "reminder" sheet.

In tournament play, use tennis web sites to scout future opponents. However, avoid talking about the opponent's rankings or past success. If possible, resist allowing your child to look at the draw; it will pull them out of their performance frame of mind. You as the parent may be able to look at the opponent's past match record and decide which style of play may work best against them. Then formulate a game plan. Identify performance goals, such as strategies and tactics and possible patterns of play.

On match days, assist them in warming up their primary and secondary strokes, make sure their nutrition and hydration needs are met, remind them to go for a short run before checking in and avoid taking naps in-between matches.

Refusing To Play Them Down, When It Might Pump Them Up!

Are you seeking to build your child's confidence, self-esteem or focus ability? Do you want to provide the crucial experience needed in order to be comfortable playing in tough finals? Playing down to pump them up is a marvelous idea. Winning a title, no matter what size, motivates them more than 20 hours of lessons.

Here's a wonderful story about how success breeds confidence. I encourage every player, in every level, who is in a rut to apply this approach.

Vania King is a former junior doubles partner of my step daughter. We had tons of fun working on the art of doubles. Vania is a motivated, persistent and hardworking tennis player. Although Vania failed to win tons of national junior titles growing up; she found tremendous confidence in a far off land. Prior to the summer national hard courts, Vania decided to try her luck in the most exotic locations in Asia. Playing the lesser events, she took the road less traveled on the ITF junior circuit.

Vania found success winning a couple minor ITF events. This sky rocked her confidence in herself! It also drew attention from the USTA, which in turn awarded her a hand full of wildcards into major WTA tour events including the U.S. Open. Armed with this new found confidence, Vania won a few rounds in the U.S. Open and by year's end found herself ranked top 50 in the world on the WTA pro tour. Sometimes playing down can pump them up!

FUN FACT: Vania went on to win the 2010 Wimbledon and US Open Women's Doubles titles.

Forgetting You Must Be Present to Win

Only by risking going too far can you find out how far your child can go!

"The draws too tough, my Kelly can't beat those girls!"; "You mean, fly to an event, I hate airports"; "We'd have to stay in a hotel and that costs money"; "We would have to drive for over an hour"; " I'd miss the Neiman Marcus sale"; "The Miami Dolphin game is Sunday!"; "I do a 30 mile bike ride on weekends"…

Champions aren't born, they are made, remember?

Here's an actual story, the names have been changed to protect the guilty mom.

Luke was on the alternate list for the Palm Springs National. Mom says, "There's no way we're driving out there. It's a two hour trek."

I plea, "But Kathy, Luke's 7 players- out of the main draw and 5 of the other players ahead of him are from back east. They won't fly out if their player's not in. Just go! Make a day of it. If he doesn't get in, stop at the Cabazon outlet malls; enjoy your family and Palm Springs. Trust me."

So, they went. Luke got in. He blew through the draw reaching the semifinals. His national ranking jumped 250 points. Luke hasn't been on the alternate list since. From then on, he not only qualifies for all the nationals, but was actually seeded in the lower level events. His confidence shot through the roof. He went on to beat players he had never beaten before. You know the saying; you have to be present to win!

Watching their Matches versus Charting and Video Taping

Smart training begins with providing valuable feedback to your child's coaches. Charting and videotaping actual matches is one of the best ways to assist your child in progressing at the quickest rate.

There are several types of charts a parent can use during an actual match. Later in this book we'll decipher each type of chart. (Part Four: Parent and Player Accountability) We'll spend some time reviewing the benefits of each.

Parents keep in mind that the most common learning style is the visual learner. Having your child sit down and review their match performance often provides valuable insight, as well as proof.

Here are a few topics to look for while reviewing the DVD: strengths and weaknesses in stroke production, shot selection, dissecting the opponent, movement, emotional and/or lapses in concentration. Trust me, break out the video camera and begin to document one match every tournament and you will be on the road to discovery.

Expecting Your Child to Win Their First Few Big Events

Remember back as a kid at Halloween; you and your friends were walking into a haunted house for the first time. You didn't really know what to expect. Your heart was racing, your palms were sweating and you were scared to death, but did your best not to show it. By the fourth or fifth time running through the same haunted house, it wasn't so scary anymore right?

It's difficult for even the best competitors to compete at their peak performance levels in this heightened state of arousal.

Explain to your child that these first few larger events are just rehearsals. This approach will de-stress your child. As a matter of fact, if your child's young enough, don't even tell them it's a higher level.

FUN FACT: The number one seed seldom wins in junior competition.

Worrying About Things Beyond Your Control

A sure way to ruin your day and jeopardize your child's success is to worry about issues beyond your control. For instance, complaining about the drive to the event, the lack of quality restaurants around the site, the lack of parking, the draw, the weather, a change in the start time, the official who doesn't pay attention, the "creative line caller", or the other crazy parents. Negative pre-match behavior influences your child's outlook, attitude and performance.

Agonizing over uncontrollable issues disturbs your peace of mind and torments those around you. Simply put, when a parent is unraveling, the player is sure to follow. Just because you are not talking about your frustrations, your negative energy and anxiety levels can be detected by all those around you.

Experienced tennis parents focus on de-stressing the environment. There is a direct link between parental composure and player composure. Pre-match conversations should be about the process of preparation – focusing on what the child can control. During the match it is the parent's role to remain calm and relaxed. Charting is a terrific way to stay busy to avoid showing emotion. Your child will look to you for comfort- a freaked out parent is not that comforting!

SPECIAL NOTE: Have you ever notice how tranquil the parents of notorious cheaters are while their child is cheating? They're as quiet as a church mouse!

FORMING POSITIVE ATTITUDES BLUNDERS

"Never outgrow fun."

Overlooking Goal Setting

Goal setting and organizing should be used as soon as your child enters into the competitive phase. After an event, plan on setting some goals as you organize their upcoming lessons. Sit down with them to review their completed match logs at an appropriate time. (Match logs are provided in Part Four.)

This analysis provides their "Blue Print" for the upcoming week's worth of lessons and clinics. Being prepared and organized promotes a positive attitude.

There are four sides to your youngster's game that needs to be developed. Put in writing the four sides of development and identify a weakness that can be improved upon.

For example:

Technical: Slice backhand

Tactical: How to beat a moonball/pusher

Movement/Fitness: Develop core strength and stability

Emotional/Focus: Practicing closing out 5-2 leads

At all levels of junior competition, matches should be viewed as an information gathering session. The overall objective is to improve every week.

FUN FACT: Top players enter an average of 35 tournaments a year and win three or four!

Outcome Oriented Questions and Negative Remarks

Asking your child "Did you win?" after each practice match or tournament match is the worst thing you could ask. Champions are performance oriented, not outcome oriented. How can we ask them to focus on simple performance goals, if you are focused only on the outcome?

Focus on saying 5 positive comments for every negative remark. Kids pick up every negative word, condescending tone of voice, upset facial expressions and defensive body language. Try to replace "Did you win?" with "Did you hit your performance goals today?"

Focusing Only on Aptitude and Overlooking Attitude

Think back to the beginning of the book. The two sides that dictate your child's development is nature (their genetic predisposition or brain type) and nurture.

Let's talk about the nurturing side.

The way you, as parents see the world greatly influences your children's view of the world. Positive minded people share a "can do" attitude. Optimism is empowering. Confidence is contagious!

Pessimistic parents nurture the blame game. Pessimists often take the victim role. I've discovered most negative people don't see themselves as pessimistic, negative or jaded. They see themselves as being unlucky, or "in reality" and optimistic folks as being "out of touch".

Wayland, the Laguna Beach artists puts it this way. "There are two types of people: "anchors and motors."

There's some good news here! The first thing is that pessimistic attitudes can be unlearned. Anchors can become motors! The second is that you can choose to avoid the poison. If anyone, including you or your spouse is toxic to the progress of your child's tennis game, it may be wise to provide that parent with an off court secondary role. For example, ask them to be the travel agent, tournament scheduling manager, racket stringer or equipment manager. These are still very important "behind the scenes" jobs.

Here's a fun saying: Attitude determines altitude even more so than aptitude. Nurturing optimism is even more important than nurturing strokes. A terrific attitude is enjoyed for a life time, on and off the court.

Assuming Your Teen is Organized and Accountable

As tennis begins to shift from a recreational sport to the competitive game it's important that all members of the family entourage understands their team duties. Drafting a family agreement is a peaceful way to "put into writing" each person's responsibilities.

Here is a Sample Agreement:

Parent agrees to financially support child's tennis career to the amount of X dollars per month, drive them to X number of lessons, clinics, practice sets, tournaments , purchase equipment, provide physical therapy…etc.

Child agrees to X numbers of off-court training hours, X-numbers of lessons and clinics, X number of practice sets….etc. If the child doesn't fulfill their requirements, all parties agree chasing the dream is over.

FUN FACT: If your child's actions do not match their words, you may have a normal child. Very few children have what it takes to be an elite national level player.

Misunderstanding Choking Under Stress

From the novice level all the way up to the ATP/WTA professional tour levels there are two opposite failures that often occur under stress: choking and panicking. They are often misdiagnosed by parents, coaches and players.

 The first failure that occurs under stress is choking: the process of over thinking. Choking usually begins when the player's mind leaves his or her performance goals and begins to obsess about the future outcome. The top players who struggle with choking often report that their head is focused on future scenarios, such as: What if I lose to this jerk? What are my friends gonna say? What's my ranking going to drop to? Where's the trophy going to go in my room? Past thoughts can also take over your child's brain at the most inopportune times. Such as: I'm going to lose. I always lose three set matches! I'm playing Kelly, she always cheats!

Over thinking occurs when your child's brain is entangled in the past or future instead of simply in the present. Without getting too technical, the left side of their brain is the ego, analytical, judgmental side that is getting in the way. The solution is giving that "left" side of the brain some all important jobs to do. The key is to keep the brain's overly judgmental or overly emotional sides busy, so it isn't left to its old sabotaging habits.

So how does your child keep their destructive side busy? The answer is employing both between point and change-over rituals.

Ask your child to play sets and rehearse focusing on exact change over rituals and between point rituals. By keeping the left side busy, so it can't pull them away from the present!

Misunderstanding Panicking Under Stress

Panicking is the second most often found emotional breakdown at all levels of the competitive game.

Panicking is the process of not thinking. After a rash of unforced errors a player may slide into an angry emotional state and choose to ignore their between point rituals. Their heart rate races and they begin playing fast, reckless, thoughtless tennis. Panicking players miss hit and give away point after point.

As a panicking player re-engages their between point rituals, they need to calm down by breathing deeply and plan on hitting 3 clean balls straight up the middle of the court. This stops the flow of unforced errors. Most champions take around 5 seconds to get over the previous point and 10 seconds to plan the next point. Simply taking 15 seconds to relax and spot tendencies is the solution that stops the panic.

Freaking Them Out Before a Final

Think back to the beginning of this year. Who won the earlier titles? Do you know? Can you remember? Come on, think hard…

Even if your little super star wins this next major event, will anyone remember in a couple of months? Probably not! Will anyone else really care? Not really.

A common blunder occurs when a child reaches a final. Parents often are to blame for making this one day, this one event, so important. This frequently adds stress and kills any chance of peak performance. I want to remind you that your child performs best when he or she is relaxed. A tennis parent's role is de-stressing their child.

Postponing Happiness

Good memories are your most valuable possessions. Impatience ruins the moment. Arriving at the top of the junior tennis world is a slow walk up a million steps, not a quick elevator ride to the top!

Some parents spend their child's whole junior career frustrated, anxious and depressed. You will too, if you dwell only on failures, problems and future concerns. Some parents postpone their happiness, gratitude and love.

> I've often heard parents say "I'll smile when she
> finally wins one!"

Enjoy the journey. Your child will be off to college sooner than you think.

FUN FACT: Half the things you worry about don't happen anyway!

ACCELERATED GROWTH BLUNDERS

"Change is the only thing that's permanent."

Not Seeing Stumbling Blocks as Stepping Stones

Here's a terrific example: a few years back, Molly Scott (former 2006, SCTA #1, Dartmouth College standout, currently on the WTA tour) sprained her non-dominant left wrist.

Her initial position was to follow protocol which was no tennis for 4-6 weeks. Molly called saying, "Frank, I have to cancel my training for 4-6 weeks because my left arm is sprained."

I said, "That's upsetting, but we needed some time to switch focus anyway. This actually fits into a new developmental plan."

"We'll begin to organize your proactive patterns and between point rituals, we'll develop your one handed slice backhand drop shot and your low, backhand volley. Let's begin today with a new 4 week crash course on lower body fitness and stamina."

Molly's voice dropped to this low, quiet depressed tone, "ooohhh....really..aahh...that's... um....super."

SPECIAL NOTE: Six weeks later Molly beat a top ten player in the nation as she applied her new found slice backhand drop shot to perfection!

Perfectionism

The most famous, beloved art on the planet isn't perfect. The Sistine Chapel isn't perfect! The best music isn't perfect. In a 1980 interview, John Lennon said he hears flaws in every Beatle recording. In a grand slam final, even the professionals don't play every point perfectly.

Pay special attention to winners versus errors. Roger Federer often shanks balls off the frame. Serena Williams often over hits and makes a rash of errors. If you or your child is still on that high horse called "perfection", jump off!

"Success is more of a function of persistence than perfection."

At every level of competition, ask your child to simply focus on winning 65 percent of the total points. To win a match comfortably, you don't have to win every point. This gives your child permission to accept a few unforced errors. Advise your youngster that it's ok to allow the opponent to have a little glory as they win some points.

Focusing Only on Strokes

Here's a statement that should be obvious by now. Knowing how to hit strokes and knowing how to win under stress are different animals. The #1 statement I hear daily from concerned tennis parents is "My child's the better player, yet they can't win!"

The solution lies in the school methodology of teaching. Here's what I mean, throughout every grade students are taught daily to shift their focus from math to science, from English to history, etc. The common blunder in tennis development is only focusing on a singular subject (fundamental stroke production) year after year. The school methodology consistently delivers well rounded young adults. Add mental training such as shot selection, emotional training such as between point rituals and watch your child flourish.

Believing Quantity of Court Time is Quality Court Time

If your child has a reoccurring nightmare of losing to pushers in tournaments, how is spending 6 hours a day drilling the ball back and forth in an academy going to help? It's not!

After tournament matches, the parent has to provide detailed information to the coach. This is done through charting or videotaping of the match.

Unless you are paying the coach to attend the match, don't expect them to know how and why your child lost. This is where the quality of the lesson versus the quantity of hours hitting comes into play. Avoiding your child's issues isn't the best plan or the wisest way to spend your money.

SPECIAL NOTE: It takes an experienced eye to actually spot and analyze your youngsters match tendencies.

Neglecting the Between Point and Change Over Rituals

"Professionals think about a hand full of thoughts a hundred times in a single match. Juniors think about a hundred different thoughts in a single match!"

Guess when the critical mental toughness issues take place? When the ball is going back and forth or between points? Between points.

Does your child have a problem with any of these? Time management, mistake management, anger management, implementing patterns, dissecting opponents, controlling their heart rate, controlling their emotions, distraction control, quieting their mind, avoiding lapses in concentration, controlling self-condemnation, self-charting and/or controlling nervousness.

If you said "yes" to any of these, your child can benefit from rituals. Most juniors copy the pros as they apply external rituals such as toweling off and looking at their strings. While these are important relaxation techniques, the real benefits of rituals lie in the internal side.

Here are two internal habits that will greatly benefit your child's mental game:

1. The first exercise is to focus on the exact internal rituals the pros use in between points. Internal rituals include: emotionally getting over the last point, strategically planning the next point's pattern, and applying relaxation ritual.

2. The second exercise is to challenge your youngster to rehearse their change over rituals. This internal focus is a two- step process. First, only think about the last 2 games. Did they win or lose? Why or why not? Step two is to pre-plan any changes as they visualize the upcoming next two games.

FUN FACT: Youngsters have to rehearse these skills in practice sets before they become comfortable enough to apply them correctly in actual tournament play.

Ignoring Their B and C Game Plans

At the competitive stage of tennis, spend a few moments to discuss your child's primary and secondary styles of play in matches. Styles include hard hitting baseliners, all court, net rushers and retrievers. In lower levels of competition, continually bringing the opponent into the net is also an effective style of play.

Set up practice sets for your child against lower level players and ask your child to rehearse their secondary styles of play. Champions have mastered more than one style.

<u>**Example:**</u>

My step- daughter played her first adult U.S. Open at age 15. In the first round, Sarah's opponent came out with her plan A (hard hitting baseliner). Sarah won the first set 6-4. At the start of the 2nd set, the opponent switched to plan B (net rusher) and Sarah went up 4-1.

The opponent then switched to plan C (moonball/pusher), Sarah's least favorite style. Sarah was amazed to see a 30 year old WTA veteran pushed her way to a $15,000 victory in the 3rd set.

SPECIAL NOTE: Moonball/pushers style never goes away, so your player had better learn to handle it!

Overlooking the Pain Principle

Remember the old saying? "If you keep on doing what you've always done, you'll keep on getting what you've always got." Players hit common walls in their development. One of those walls is resisting change.

If your child view's change, as more painful than losing, they'll continue in the same losing path. It's so painful for some to change a flawed grip, stroke or stance; they'd rather accept the pain of losing than deal with changing.

Great things begin to happen when the pain of losing starts to be more powerful than the pain of changing. Once they accept the fact that a change has to be made, they are on their way to the next level. This is where great parenting comes in.

The cycle of change is a three step process:

1. Step one is accepting change.

2. Step two is uncomfortable because they have left their old strokes and their new strokes are not fully formed.

3. Step three is a 4-6 week developmental cycle. During this phase, their new motor programs become personalized and over-ride the old motor programs.

NOTE: At stage 2, the pain of being uncomfortable often pulls them back to their old strokes.

SPECIAL NOTE: Placing your youngster into a competitive situation before the three phases are complete may destroy their new motor program and the old strokes will surely return.

Assuming that Tennis Speed is Only Foot Speed

Tennis specific speed-training requires a combination of foot speed and anticipatory speed.

Heredity plays an important role in your child's muscle type. Simply put, some humans are born with more fast-twitch muscle fibers. Parents and coaches can't improve the genetic predisposition of an athlete, but they can nurture both their foot speed and anticipatory speed. The path to better court coverage lies in avoiding hesitation and anticipating situations.

Anticipatory speed is greatly increased by understanding and rehearsing the art of vision control. Here's a sports myth "keep your eye on the ball." I suggest shifting focus from narrow vision (watching an incoming ball) to broad vision. Broad vision is picking up visual clues as the ball travels toward the opponent. (We'll be discussing this issue in detail later in the book.)

Your child doesn't have to be the fastest runner on the court if they develop their anticipatory skills. Just ask one of my all-time favorites, former #1 Lindsey Davenport.

INTELLIGENT TRAINING BLUNDERS

"The more you know, the less you fear"

Not Having an Entourage

Youngsters that improve at the quickest rate have a full entourage. This includes private hitters, technical teachers, mental/emotional coaches, off-court trainers and clinics.

Customizing the style of coach to your player is important. Choose wisely because the two leading influences are you and the coaches you hire!

Being Oblivious to Periodization

Parents are often so blinded by winning that they unknowingly sabotage their child's success. This is especially true in the beginner and intermediate levels of competition. Understanding when to train the different elements of your child's game is called periodization. It's based on the upcoming tournament schedule.

For example: Asking your child to bulk up in the gym, run five miles, or to dismantle and fix a flawed stroke a day or two before a big event are samples of poor periodization training. Adding an unfamiliar element the day of a match also falls into this category. Unfamiliar examples may include: Indian buffet for lunch, different grip, new type of strings or an uncomfortable outfit.

SPECIAL NOTE: An essential parental skill is choosing your battles. It is important to understand when to put your foot down and pick a battle. Starting a war right before a scheduled lesson will pull your child into the wrong mental state and surely destroy any hopes of a productive session. It is also a waste of your money.

Likewise, choosing to battle the day of a scheduled match is a sure fire way to drain your youngster's emotional batteries and sabotage the actual peak performance you are seeking.

Neglecting Smart Work

Great coaches have the ability to zero in on players weakness long before players or parents even know it exist. This is where smart work comes into play.

Up to this point, we have touched on the subject of proper training, but fixing what actually needs to be fixed is crucial if you want your child to improve at the fastest rate.

Let's use an analogy, if a race car continually loses race after race due to its tires blowing out, is spending 4 hours a day polishing the fenders going to solve the problem? Not likely!

As I travel across the world conducting tennis workshops, I often see wonderful hitting pros playing "catch" with their students as they rally back and forth to each other. They are grooving primary strokes for hours on end.

While grooving is important, winning tennis is more of a game of "keep away" than "catch." Smart work would be to replace some of those hours playing "catch" with "keep away" patterns.

Your child may be working hard 4 hours a day, heck maybe even 6 hours, but is it smart work? Are you spending your limited time and money wisely?

FYI: Be prepared for your child to come home grumpy, when you ask your child's coach to begin playing "keep away" in practice versus playing "catch."

Encouraging "One Set Wonders"

First of all, I congratulate any juniors that actually play full practice matches. Across the country, most juniors hit for 20 minutes, maybe finish a set and then leave. They become accustom to being "one set wonders!" This is especially true in the intermediate levels of junior tennis.

Winning those tough three set tournament matches require practicing whole matches! Rehearsing the art of closing out full matches versus a single set will improve their mental toughness. If time is of the essence, I recommend that players play 3-sets, starting at 2-2 instead of the typical one set routine. Handling the stress of closing out the set is a big advantage. There is a huge difference between mechanical confidence and competitive confidence.

FUN FACT: To win a typical level 3 National event in the US, a player essentially has to win 5 matches. When was the last time your child honestly competed for 10-12 full sets in a 5 day period? If your child enjoys doubles, make it 20-24 sets in one week.

Putting Them in the Crowd to Get Ahead of the Crowd?

In my opinion, group clinics, or academies are terrific for intermediate players seeking repetition, socialization and tons of fun. Although it may be cheaper, large group training isn't always in your best developmental interest.

The top players spend about 20 percent of their time in group situations. Top players at an academy usually are sparing or working with a private coach. When is that last time you saw a phenom in a large group standing in line to hit one forehand every five minutes?

"To get your child ahead of the crowd, why would you put them in the crowd?"

Believing Weekly Lessons are Enough

I teach two families from Los Angeles. Both families come for 2 hours of private lessons each week. That's where the similarities end.

The parents hold opposing views on how to raise a tennis champion. The Johnsons believe that they need to make their 12 year old Kelli 100 percent self-sufficient. Mrs. Johnson says "It's up to her to do it, I can't force her." As a result, Kelly hits about two hours a week.

Mr. Asari believes that no one gets famous all by themselves. He and his son spend approximately 15 hours on the ball machine, playing practice sets, serving baskets, going for runs, hitting the gym and watching tennis on TV. They both get the same 2 hours worth of weekly lesson. The critical factor in the formula is not the lesson, but what the parents choose to do weekly around that lesson.

FUN FACT: The parents who see it as their responsibility to actively stay engaged consistently have higher ranked children, all the trophies, and all the college scholarship offers.

Going Into Battle Unprepared

Preparing for a tennis tournament is twofold. First, your child should consistently train properly a month or so before a big event. Secondly, they should have a pre-game set of rituals to assist them in their match preparation.

Hours before a match, Nadal morphs into a different personality. Chris Evert said she wouldn't even call a friend before a match in fear that it may break her concentration. Before each concert, Tom Petty sits quietly alone with his acoustic guitar visualizing and preparing for that nights concert.

Preparing mind, body and soul before a match is a learned behavior. Allowing your son to go wrestle in the grass with the other kids before a big match isn't in his best interest. Allowing your daughter to text 39 friends then fight with her boyfriend hours before a big match isn't in her best interest.

Knowing how and when to turn on the competitor within is critical. Assist your child in finding their own unique game day rituals. After the match is complete, your child can leave it all behind with no regrets.

PART FOUR:

COMMON QUESTIONS
& SOLUTIONS

ORGANIZATIONAL ISSUES

In this section, we will bring light to the mysterious, we will focus the blurry and we will answer the tough questions emailed from parents just like you from around the world!

"Planning the future saves you from regretting the past."

How do we find the right professional?

Initial instructors are usually chosen by proximity, cost and availability. Once your youngster moves into the competitive stage, it's time to identify the styles and personalities of coaches that fit your child's needs. Yes, it is perfectly acceptable to have more than one coach.

On a personal note: I taught my step daughter as a 10 year old beginner to playing in the U.S. Open. Did she do it alone?

No way. We employed several wonderful hitters throughout her development. Vic Braden was always there to help with her with her emotional side. I directed great individuals to assist our team every year for specific reasons. It was a team effort all the way. I teach 30-40 top ranked U.S. Juniors weekly and I cannot think of one contender that does not have multiple coaches.

Another great example is ATP star Sam Querrey. When I worked with Sam through his early teens we focused on the mental/emotional side of his development. His parents Chris and Mike always employed a terrific team of hitters, coaches and clinics to provide world class instruction for their son.

Here are eight types of coaches that you may be employing along your journey:

1) The Detailed, Analyzer

2) The Off Court Fitness Expert

3) The Kind and Fun Loving Coach

4) The Hitter

5) The Emotional, Psychological Coach

6) The Strategizer

7) The Academy Recruiter

8) The Drill Sergeant

Facts to Consider When Selecting a Pro

Finding a Pro is easy. Finding the right Pro may require a little thought and leg work. You may be using different types of Pros for different reasons.

Here are a few secrets to watch out for when selecting a Pro:

- Only a small hand full of pros actually teach the top players.

- Look for a coach who's enjoying what they do, it's contagious.

- Seek out a Pro that is so busy, that they don't need you.

- The 10,000 hour rule applies! Being a master coach is a learned experience.

- Seek out a Pro who understands your child's unique Brain and Body Type (Genetic Predisposition).

- Make sure the coach is asking questions, customizing and targeting their lessons.

- Contact designated and national tournament directors in your area. They know who produces champions.

- Ask every player that beats your kid, "Great match...who is your coach? Where do you train?"

- Ask a prospective coach, "We've heard great things about you, May we come and observe a few of your lessons?"

- Knowledge, love for the game and forming a connection with each student is key.

- Pay the coach to chart a match and devise his game plan for improvement. Meet regarding his observations and suggestions.

- Ask for a resume and who they trained under.

- Look for a coach that encourages independent thinking versus dependent thinking.

- Be careful, a former ATP/WTA challenger player does not always translate into a great teacher. The most successful tennis coaches were not the most successful tour players. Examples: Braden, Lansdorp and Bollettieri

- Be wary of a Pro that discourages you from hitting with other Pro's, hitters or trainers!

SPECIAL NOTE: To avoid confusion, employ one coach per job at any given time. Two different coaches employed to fix a serve may prove to be extremely confusing for your child. Conflicting information and battling egos spells trouble!

Coaching Philosophies

Larisa Prebrazhenskava is in her seventies. She coaches at the Spartak Tennis Club in Moscow, Russia. Spartak is a tiny one-court indoor beaten down facility. Larisa demands that all her player's shadow swing without touching a ball for hours on end. Her junior competitors don't take private lessons. None of Larisa's students are even permitted to play a tournament for the first three years of their development. Obviously, nurturing proper technique over fun is a corner stone of her teaching philosophy. Does this system jive with your parental philosophy?

Is it successful in her world?

Guess what ATP and WTA stars Dmitry Tursunov, Mikhail Youzhny, Dirara Safina, Elena Dementieva, Anastasia Myskina, Marot Safin, or Anna Kournikova all have in common? You guessed it. They all came out of that dingy one-court facility under the guidance of Larisa Prebrazhenskava! Larisa's passion and persistence obviously created a perfect storm to motivate players to greatness. Does Larisa's philosophy gel with your parental philosophy?

The XYZ Tennis Academy has offered us a scholarship, should we take it?

This is a touchy subject. Some of my best friends and lifelong business partners run successful academies. I am often presented business plans to open a full time academy, but I am convinced that a new blueprint is needed to ensure that each student is receiving the customized attention he/she deserves. I've opened and directed clubs and academies since the mid 1980's. These include Vic Braden Tennis Colleges, the Rancho San Clemente Tennis Club and the Sherwood Country Club- some of Southern California's most prestigious clubs. As a result, academies are very familiar territory.

FUN FACT: Since closing my academy and opening The Mental, Emotional Tennis Workshops our players have won 77 U.S. National singles titles since 2003.

Here are my feelings toward academies in this stage in my coaching career.

The Positive Side:

- Academies provide a terrific social environment for the players. The players can hang out with their peers of both genders.

- Players can experience the bonding of a team versus the individualism the sport often requires.

- A few top players receive free t-shirts, bags and sweats with the academies logo. Other players may receive a discount.

- Academies provide a convenient one-stop shop for parents. In essence, the parents can rely on others to organize and develop their child's career.

- Academies should provide plenty of free hitting, off-court training options and match play for the motivated individuals.

- Live ball sparring. Players grow from the daily battle.

- Academies get players good. How good? With the rare exception, most attendees advance to high school varsity, top sectionally ranked and/or NAIA to Division 2-3 level college ball.

- Players experience many different coaches and coaching styles.

FUN FACT: Most juniors are not truly interested in putting the hard work it requires to be a national champion. They are hobbyist. In that situation, academies could be the right choice. Remember, tennis is a terrific hobby.

SPECIAL NOTE: If your child is ranked higher than most players in the academy, you may be able to negotiate attending for FREE in exchange for attracting paying customers to the program. Also, some academies give every attendee a price break thus giving everyone a partial scholarship. That is, if you pay up front! Folks, that's marketing 101.

The Negative Side:

- Most academies recruit their top players AFTER a quality teacher has developed the student's skills.

- The paying customer should receive instruction equal to that given to the elite superstars, which attend for FREE. Unfortunately, in some cases, the experienced coaches are busy working privately with the non paying super stars and NOT with your child.

- In the higher levels of high performance tennis, detailed customization of the lesson plans are required. For example, if a player has holes in their transition game, sending them down to court #6 to get in line with the rest of the group and hit forehands and backhands may not be in the student's best interest.

- Paying customers do not progress at the quickest rate. Often they have to win to move up into the "higher" level courts. This forces the junior to choose outcome goals over performance goals. This means they avoid building their new weapons as they choose to use their old comfortable "flawed strokes" to try to win. This behavior stalls the exact progression you seek.

- A great young talent positioned in an unsupervised setting will often learn how to goof off, throw their racquet, waist time, go for low percentage shots, over hit, and give half effort.

- Often inexpensive overworked introductory coaches are employed to oversee the paying customers.

FUN FACT: In the last decade, most park & rec's, high school courts, apartment complex, college courts, country club and city facility have changed the name of their after school junior tennis program to an academy. It sounds more official, doesn't it?

Mental & Emotional Tennis Myths of Junior Competition

It's such a crazy world spending everyday with ranked juniors. Deciphering the facts from the myths raises a handful of question. Their attitudes and points of view of the game never cease to amaze me. They tend to be so unevenly developed. On court, they handle more pressure than most adults I know. Off-court, it is often a very different story. I know a 22 year old top 80, WTA tour player who is socially inept. Sadly, she watches cartoons for hours on end in her down time.

Below are some of the "Best Tennis Myths" coming out of the mouths of your kids!

When I Become a Pro: Then I'll Train like a Pro
Professionals have to "live the life" for years before they actually win a single match on tour. The formula is 20 hours a week for 10 years to compete on the ATP or WTA level. Begin by challenging your child to train 20 hours a week for a month.

I Need More…More is Better
In matches, most juniors think about too many things. They have a tendency to over-hit; their body is off balance at contact as opposing force vectors fly in all directions; their racquet head is rolling through the hitting zone and their running through four segment swings. The key is to simplify. Most often, improving is about "trimming the fat" not adding more.

I Will Just "Wing It" Later
Planning reduces your stress. Often we see players begin to pack their racquets, find a new outfit, clean their water bottles, search for their over grips, print out the directions to the site, look up their opponent record, make breakfast, take a shower, brush their teeth all within the last 10 minutes before they are scheduled to leave. Hum…no wonder they're angry and stressed.

I Played a Set Last Week, I'm Fine
To win major events you must be a good finisher. Building a tract record of closing out matches is the key. Exchange playing a set with playing 2 out of 3 sets and finish the match. The most important stage of any set is the end! If time is short, start each set at 2-2 but close out sets. On practice days, professional's close out 2-4 sets a day.

I Can't Control My Anger or My Wandering Mind
Re-programming these dominant thoughts takes about four to six weeks of serious focused attention. It's often the same program as rebuilding a flawed stroke. Remember discussing this topic in the blunder section? You've built up that negative path. Retooling your emotions and thoughts on court is a learned behavior. The only way to break a bad habit is to replace it with a "stronger" good habit.

To be Great, I Have to Play at My Peak Everyday
Peak level and peak efforts are two different elements. It is too taxing to be physically, mentally, spiritually and emotionally ready to battle everyday of their lives. Training in intervals is called periodization. After a tournament you should "unplug". That's right, recharge the batteries. In the practice phase strive for peak effort and let go of peak performance.

If you're Laughing, You're not Working Hard Enough
When you laugh, dance, smile or even hug someone you get biochemical surges of positive energy. Neuroscience studies clearly show that when you smile and laugh you stay in the correct (right) side of your brain. This is where muscles flow effortlessly and great decisions are made quickly. When you're

mad, judgmental or over analytical the right side of your brain shuts down and you are toast!

Don't Look Bad, Just be Cool and Play Safe On-Court!
Right around high school children begin to fear what others might think. Their mission shifts into this crazy mode, just make it look close or just don't embarrass yourself mode. So on-court, they "push the ball" under stress and play "not to look bad" instead of playing to win. If you're afraid to look bad, you are not going to enjoy peak performance. Champs play to win. Either way, win or lose, winners play to win!

My Competitors are my Enemies: I don't talk to any of them!

I admit the tennis world can be a difficult world to live in. Surviving it and rising above it requires networking and relationships. Befriending your competitors may lead to new opportunities and growth.

The following are examples of the possible benefits of befriending competitors:

- Their coach may relate to you better than your coach?

- They may have a great internet travel site or know of a hotel that has awesome practice courts at the next tournament?

- Possibly you may need a warm up partner at next week's national event.

- Practicing with your enemies gets you used to the stress of being on court with them.

- Just maybe, the player that you thought was "perfect" was actually clueless!

- It's possible that they are playing a future tournament that you did not know about?

- What if you need a doubles partner in the upcoming doubles championships?

- A competitor may know the current crop of USTA high performance coaches that you should get to know if you are interested in applying for wild cards into Pro events? So Mingle and Network.

What Does a Top Player's Weekly Training Schedule Look Like?

I encourage parents to customize the training to the player's needs. Your youngster's requirements will dramatically vary from age divisions, maturity levels, and how well they digest information.

Training regiments also vary depending on the upcoming tournament schedule. Obviously a player in the semi -finals of a big event would train radically different than a player two weeks away from their next tournament/team match.

Assisting your child in organizing their weekly schedule is one of the most important jobs of a tennis parent. This time management skill will prepare them for life on and off the courts. Also, it's important to remember the success formula to becoming world class: Twenty hours a week for about ten years. (You should have it memorized by now.)

The following is a sample week of one of our top nationally ranked U.S. Juniors. His long term goal is to play division 1 college tennis and then progress to the pro tours.

SAMPLE TRAINING WEEK	
Training /Hours	Training Example
Practice Sets/Tournament Matches: 4 Hours	It's important to schedule different styles and different ability levels of opponents.
Technical Lessons: 2 Hours	Correct flaws in their primary strokes and begin to build their secondary strokes.
Mental & Emotional Training: 4 Hours	Focus on between point rituals as well as pro active patterns to beat the 3 styles of opponents.
Video Analysis: 1 Hour	Video tape a tournament match, then have a pro do a video analysis lesson. Chart to spot tendencies.
Off-Court Gym: 3 Hours	Core and upper body strength is more important than ever. Hit the gym to prevent injuries as well as build muscle mass.
Off-Court Cardio: 4 Hours	Cross train with short sprints, up hills. Use a random directional approach to clean up hesitation.
Watching Tennis on TV: 2 Hours	Chart the pros, spot styles of play, analyze footwork, and decipher patterns and tendencies of players.
TOTAL TRAINING IN ONE WEEK: 20 HOURS	

Nurturing parents wants to provide every opportunity for their children. That's common around the globe. Most parents and players aren't interested in attaining world class levels. However, I've yet to have a parent come to me and state "my wife and I want you to train our daughter to be a completely average tennis player."

If you want to provide every opportunity to your child, I recommend picking up a weekly planner at an office store.

Ask your child to document their school, homework and tennis schedule each week. Even at the beginning levels of competition, discipline your child to actually complete a weekly planner and be accountable for their time and actions. Time management skills are essential life lessons.

How do we plan our child's tournament schedule?

One of the first things I recommend at the start of a new year is to prepare a tournament schedule. Break it down quarterly. Having your child's short and long term goals in mind is an important start. Different goals would suggest different scheduling.

For example, if your child is seeking a division 1 college tennis scholarship, I would recommend skipping high school tennis or playing a modified I.T.F. schedule. College coaches are most eager to recruit nationally ranked players. They don't consider high school tennis as high performance.

Is having your child ranked in the boys 10's your goal? Is developing your daughter's game to compete on the pro tours the goal? These very different long term goals require very different training and tournament scheduling.

Once a player reaches their early teens and they are technically sound, the technical training of the player becomes a little less important. What begins to come into play is the focus on the physical, mental and emotional training as well as the organization of the player's training and competitive scheduling.

The important factors to consider when planning an optimal competitive schedule are:

Your Child's Age:
The age eligibility requirements in different USTA sections. Some countries limit the number of events a junior can participate in each age division. Customize your child's stay in each division to maximize rankings and exposure to prospective college recruiters.

Also, consider your child's win-loss ratio in each division. In my opinion, a child should stay in their current division if they are winning around 70% of their matches. With that said, losing approximately 50% of tournament matches would suggest scaling back a level. While winning 80-90% of their matches may suggest moving up a division or age bracket.

The Type of Tournament to Play:
Plan on mixing lower level, your child's current level and higher level events into the tournament schedule. In my opinion, nothing breeds confidence like winning trophies. So enter your child into events they can do well in. It may be in your child's best interest for you to merge court surface events together for maximum results. For example: Book a smaller clay court event the week before the clay court nationals and/or encourage your child to play doubles in tournament events. Doubles require a different set of skills (Both tennis and personal skills).

Two Weeks On and One Week Off:
I recommend this formula while scheduling. It allows for competitive play as well as down time to fix flaws, re-charge batteries and heal injuries. Occasionally, travel expenses dictate that your child stay on the tournament trail longer.

Your Family's Economics:
Here in the US, hospitality options are rare. In Europe, there is a host family waiting with room and board for the player and coach at each event. I recommend calling the tournament director to inquire about it. Parents need to factor in the expenses of gear, clothes, training, flights, parking, rental cars, hotels, food and beverages.

Your Child's Educational Commitments:
Consider your child's school commitments. Factor in final tests and exams. National events and exams all seem to fall around holiday breaks.

Your Child's Fitness Level:
Remember the ever ready battery "takes a licking and keeps on ticking." Well, that may or may not be your child. Having the physical batteries to play two matches a day for weeks on end may be a bit much to ask of your player. Even the top professionals are not competing two singles matches a day for three weeks straight!

Your Child's Tolerance Levels:
Emotional tolerance and frustration tolerance is worth looking into. Keep in mind that every round your child marches through the draw, half the players lose. Pressure and stress can often double or triple. What is your child's frustration tolerance level?

Your Child's Ranking Goals:
Here's a formula to increase your child's national ranking. Year in and year out, certain level 2 national events draw the top field of 64 players in your child's current division. Occasionally 58 out of the 64 players are ranked higher and are presumably stronger than your child. What are the actual chances of getting deep into the draw and collecting those precious national points? Often, during the same week, another level 2 national event (same points available) is being held in a less desirable city. By checking the internet, you'll notice that historically some tournaments draw a lower level field. My suggestion is to go there. By playing the ranking game your child's national ranking will begin to sky- rocket.

In scheduling practice sets, what should my daughter focus on?

FUN FACT: Top players preparing for a big event usually do "twofers!" that is, they train twice a day. One session is 2.5 hours of drills, patterns, off-court training. The other session is 2.5 hours of sets. Most players focus on winning. I believe in focusing on improving!

Design a plan of action, a focal point for each day's practice session. By far, the most important issue is playing their game. (Does your player know what their game is?) That means exposing their strengths, hiding their weakness and running their best patterns to perfection. In essence, it's about pulling the opponent into their best style of tennis. Small adaptations, as well as complete different tactical approaches, are needed to be developed.

Place a check mark next to any of the below common issues that you would classify as one of your youngsters reoccurring nightmares. Reoccurring nightmares are issues that breakdown in match play tournament after tournament.

Below are 20 common topics to focus on during practice sets:

1) **How to Beat Moonball/Pusher/Retrievers**

    Why: To build the mental/emotional tools required to overcome a world class pusher. Ask your child to incorporate short angle patterns, moonball approach shot to swing volley patterns and drop shot patterns to pull the opponent into uncomfortable territory.

2) **How to Beat Hard Hitting Baseliners**

    Why: To build the tools required to take a hard hitter out of their game. Do so by asking your child to mix the spin, speed and trajectories. Also, focus on achieving 65 percent first serves percentage as well as consistent depth on ground strokes.

3) How to Beat All Court/Net Rushers

Why: To rehearse the patterns and plays used to keep them away from the net. Two initial ways to keep a solid net rusher away from the net are once again the 65 percent serving rule and the "deep groundies" rule. Also, devote time rehearsing capturing the net first. The function here is forcing them to play behind the court where they are often more uncomfortable.

4) Focus Only on Serve Patterns

Why: To develop the variation of shot sequences used by top servers. Pattern repetition is an important missing link in most junior's development. Ask them to play a set while only being concerned with their consistent wide serve patterns. The next sets ask them to focus their attention on serving patterns up the center.

5) Focus Only on the Return of Serve Pattern

Why: To develop the different return positions and types of return patterns. Top players employ three positions while returning serve. Eight feet behind the court while arching a building shot, on the baseline using a solid ground stroke and inside the court applying a visual distraction and reducing the server's time on their first ground stroke.

6) Focus Only on the Rally Patterns

Why: To rehearse how to expose their strengths and hide their weaknesses in a rally. Ask your child to give attention to the proper height over the net from various positions. Invite your child to focus on the zone in which each ball lands. Run their "side door" short angle patterns. Apply isolating the opponent's weaker side until they get the desired short ball.

7) **Focus Only on the Net Rushing Patterns**

Why: To rehearse tactics used to capture the net. Ask your child to devote time to tactics such as serve and volley, chip and charge, apply their moonball approach to swing volleys. Top players also spot the opponent's vulnerable "one-segment" swing (defensive slice) and steal the volley!

8) **Focus Spotting and Applying Offense, Neutral, and Defensive Shot Selections**

Why: Understanding these principles will reduce errors and manage the time between hits in a rally. Where the incoming ball is about to land on your child's side of the court dictates their shot selection options.

FUN FACT: As coaches, we often divide the court into three zones. From the net to the service line is called the kill or offensive zone. From the service line to about half way back towards the baseline is the building or neutral zone. The remaining 4-5 feet of court closest to the baseline is the defensive zone. Most errors in high level tennis stem from poor shot selection choices.

9) **Focus on Spotting Game Points (Mega Points) as well as the Hidden Mini Mega Points**

Why: Controlling the big points requires that you spot them first. Mega points are any game winning points. They require your full attention. Mini mega points are 30-15. They also require your full attention. Win it and you've established a comfortable 40-15 lead. Lose it and its 30-30.

Discuss the different strategic approaches to a positive mega point versus a negative mega point. Shot selection choices are quite opposite given a 40-15 "positive" mega point versus a 15-40 "negative" mega point.

The same mini mega principle applies to games as well. Think about breaking your opponents serve to gain a 4-2 lead in the set. Win the next game and it's 5-2. Lose it and its 4-3. There's a mental, emotional edge that comes with adding extra pressure on an opponent at the right time. Ask your child to simply begin to spot these critical points in their practice sets.

10) **Focus on Rehearsing Proper Between Point Rituals and Change Over Rituals**

Why: Strategies, tactics, emotional and focus control are all done in between points. It's estimated that 25 percent of the time that you're on the court you're in a point. 75 percent of the time you're in these between point stages. That's a staggering amount of time.

Rehearse sets using the three stages of between point rituals (Get over the last point, plan the next point's pattern and relaxation ritual). Also, during changeovers, only be concerned with thinking two games back and two games forward. This will keep your attention in the present. Allowing your mind to wonder to the past or future is detrimental to your performance goals.

11) **Self-Chart Both Players: Errors to Winners**

Why: To understand when, where and why winners and errors are occurring. We call it spotting tendencies. Often during the change over's during practice sets, I'll ask our players "Is your opponent committing more forehand or backhand errors?" or "Where are you committing most of your errors?" The typical answer is " Ahhh..I dunno!"

Ask your child to devote a few minutes in between practice games to remain aware of the errors to winners and spotting patterns. The smart player keeps track. If your child can get used to playing and thinking, they'll have a monumental advantage when tournament sets go to a tie breaker!

12) Focus Control: Broad Versus Narrow Vision

Why: It develops quicker anticipatory speed, court coverage, court awareness. Narrow vision is used when the incoming ball is approaching your child. Their attention should be on watching the ball after the bounce in their strike zone.

FUN FACT: Avoid asking them to watch it hit their racket. Kids are smart. You'll be embarrassed. No human can actually see a 2-3 millisecond event.

Broad vision is employed when the ball has left your child's strings and is out bound towards the opponent's side. Ask your child to shift their focus to the big picture. They'll need to spot where their ball is about to land, their opponent's court position, their swing speed and swing length and their probable strike zone.

If they sense the opponent is on defense, they should be moving to an offensive position. On the other side, if they spot the opponent moving forward preparing to cream the ball, your child should be preparing for defense.

Good players have fast reaction time. They possess quick hands and fast feet. Great players have those skills as well as anticipation. Average players focus on simply tracking the ball. Advanced players pick up visual clues milliseconds before the opponent strikes the ball. Top players position themselves based on the pre-strike observations of the opponent.

Examples include:

A.) Watching the knee, hip and shoulder rotation as well as the ball toss angle before the opponent serves. Can you spot the obvious ball toss of a kick serve?

B.) Watching the shoulder position and racket face angle before an opponent volleys. Can you read a crosscourt versus down the line incoming volley?

C.) Watching the flight pattern, swing speed and swing length of the opponent's backswing on their ground strokes. Can you spot a slice backhand versus top spin backhand before the opponent strikes the ball?

FUN FACT: Top players aren't always faster; they simply understand what they are seeing and adjust quicker than the average player.

13) **Be a Hard Hitting Baseliner**

Why: Rehearse the patterns used by this style of play. Position yourself close to the baseline and enjoy reducing their recovery time. Crush every short ball and wear the opponent down by torturing them east coast to west coast.

14) **Be a Moonball/Pusher/Retriever**

Why: Most juniors are hard hitting baseliners. Guess which style they hate to play the most? Pushers! Position yourself farther back into a defensive mode. Enjoy watching them self-destruct. Feel like the longer the rally, the better.

15) **Be an All Court/Net Rusher**

Why: Having a solid plan B or C game plan is the difference in winning whole tournaments. Enjoy shortening the points - Apply pressure by forcing your way into the net. Show your athleticism by using your quick reflex volleys and smashes.

16) Play with Only a Slice Backhand

Why: Isolating this shot will force you to practice it. It will also develop the skills of running around the backhand to punish the inside out forehand.

17) Play with Only a Second Serve

Why: Rehearse the physical/mental/emotional tools required to compete when your first serve is not working. You'll need to utilize kick and slice second serves in the higher levels.

18) Play with Only Wide Serves or Down the "T" Serves

Why: In order to control the court, you must be able to serve to their weaker side. Pattern rehearsal is the next step after you are comfortable with your fundamental strokes. Holding serve requires an arsenal of serving patterns.

19) Continually Mix the Spins, Speeds and Trajectory of the Ball

Why: Hard hitting baseliners and "wristy" players will make a lot of errors if you can mix up your shots. Also, most top juniors rally with their hitting coach for hours a day. If you hit the opponent the same type of ball that they see day in day out, you are giving them what they love and you " ain't a gonna" win.

20) Play Mega Point Sets "Win 3 Points in a Row" Scoring

Why: Focus control. Most of us win a point...then give one back!

SPECIAL BONUS: Spot and Attack the "One Segment Swing"

Why: An opponent is in a vulnerable position when they are unable to set up and uncoil the kinetic chain. It looks like a defensive slice ground stroke. Spot it and attack when they are vulnerable. As you can see, there's a reason why it takes years to be world class. Plan on spending a minimum of two months on this topic alone!

My Mom only wants me to play better players and then always goes psycho when I lose! Is this right?

Most junior tennis players and their parents fall into the trap of ONLY seeking "up" matches. Up matches or playing someone better is a terrific way for your child to rehearse their A game plan. It can provide a major confidence boost to hold your own or even take a set from a higher level player. It's a prominent way to get pushed and stretched to the limit.

However, beware of two pitfalls. One is that your child will lose most of the time and that isn't always the best way to motivate some brain types. Second, be aware that it may be a false victory! A false victory is achieved when the higher level opponent isn't trying to win, but is using your child as a sparring partner to rehearse his or her B or C game plans, secondary strokes or patterns. I often ask my players to play lesser players and focus on only hitting slice backhands. They are not trying to win at all.

Alexa Glatch is a great Southern California player. She is highly ranked on the WTA tours and has played on the U.S. Federation Cup squad. All through her junior career we scheduled sparring matches. She would be absolutely ok with losing most of the practice matches as she rehearsed her weaker proactive patterns or her secondary strokes that she didn't quite own. The other top 10 nationally ranked juniors wouldn't dare rehearse their weaker patterns and plays because they were obsessed with having to win on the practice court.

FUN FACT: Each player that beat Alexa on the practice court played division 1 college ball, while Alexa enjoyed life traveling the world on the on the WTA pro tour.

I suggest asking your child to spend an equal amount of time playing weaker players. This will assist in the development of their B and C game plans. We know that players need to master different styles of play in order to be a contender at the national level.

Juniors, quite honestly, won't even try to develop their B and C game in an up practice match. (They don't want to lose at a faster rate. Can you blame them?) If they won't rehearse those skills in an up practice match ...and they do not want to play practice sets against weaker opponents...when will the skills be developed and rehearsed?

The interesting question is: Why won't your child play players they speculate are worse? Usually it is a genuine fear of an ego whipping.

SPECIAL NOTE: Players that won't play down practice matches can often blame their parent's fragile ego. Uneducated parents unknowingly sabotage their child's growth by not allowing them to play sets versus different styles and levels of opponents.

At our workshops, we structure practice sets against different styles of opponents, not just different levels. If your child has issues beating a Moonball/Pusher... guess what we focus on? You guessed it, the tools required to beat a Moonball/Pusher! Also, we gladly assist players in finding a weekly up match as long as they agree to play a down match as well.

Even after a practice set, the first thing my Dad asks me is "Did You Win?"

I must say, this is the single most reported stressor that talented juniors have to deal with. This mind set often comes from uninformed parents. It's sure to stunt any child's growth.

It's the parental job to shift the child's focus from outcome goals to performance goals. On any given Saturday here in Southern California, a typical girls 14's designated open tournament has 250 participants. One goes home a winner. Two hundred forty nine go home losers.

Everyone's primary objective is to win. The champions are the ones who focus on the performance goals versus the winning or losing. Parents have to lead the way in focusing on performance goals. The players who can focus on the tactics and patterns are the ones who usually come out on top.

Should my son copy Nadal?

Before I answer this question, let's review some of the facts I love about Rafael Nadal...and you should too.

- His Uncle taught him how to play. They've stuck together as a team. That's respectful.

- At 14, The Spanish Federation invited him to train in Barcelona, essentially, taking over his training. He already had a great team so he declined. That's loyalty.

- As a youngster, his emotions were like a volcano, so his uncle made him play with dead balls and inferior gear to teach him how to deal with adversity. That builds character.

- Nadal has an entourage: His coaches (Tony Nadal and Francisco Roig), his trainer and his hitter (Marc Lopez). That's smart!

- Nadal has a pre match routine that he uses before every match: He gets to the site a few hours early to warm up on a side court, he showers, eats, then gets taped up; He plays the match in his head (visualization) a half hour before it begins, he puts on his favorite Spanish pop music and then The Phantom of The Opera on his i-Pod, he jogs, jumps in place and builds a sweat while visualizing his performance goals. Great preparation- that's comforting.

- Nadal's focus is on the need to improve versus the need to win. Rafa was quoted as saying "To improve you have to make mistakes. That's the problem with improving, you have to accept this."That's intelligent!

- In early 2008 at #2 in the world, Uncle Tony decided that Rafa needed to improve his offensive court position to win major hard and grass court events. For months, they worked on positioning on the baseline, taking balls early and stealing volleys. He went from being a retriever to a counter puncher, to an attacker. Rafa's insight, knowing he could still improve, yielded him an Olympic gold, a Wimbledon Championship and the world's #1 ranking. That's brilliant!

- Rafa has had more than his share of injuries yet comes back stronger than ever. That's character! (2004- a stress fracture took him off the court for 3 months; 2005- a mysterious foot injury sidelined him for months; 2009- knee tendentious took him out for 2 months.)

- Rafa is a well-rounded person who has outside interests and hobbies. He can be found enjoying golf and fishing on his days off. He also champions his own charity foundation called Fundacion RafaNadal. That's honorable!

- Rafa is disciplined. The next step after motivation is discipline. He does what he has to do when he has to do it. No excuses, no procrastination. That's fixation.

How Can Your Child Attain Rafa's Top 10 Tools:

1) Hit the gym to gain brute strength.

2) Commit to improving with unrelenting determination.

3) Develop the mental side of shot selection to master offense, neutral & defensive skills.

4) Schedule time to strengthen their speed, stamina, and agility.

5) Revise their between point rituals to enhance their "clear headedness" of shot selection on big points.

6) Upgrade their ability to apply spin.

   FUN FACT: Average ball rotation off Agassi's forehand: 1800 rpm's, Federer's forehand: 2500 rpm, Nadal's forehand: 3200 rpm's

7) Cultivate the competitive attitude. Do this by adding simulated stress with every drill. We call them "stress buster drills."

8) Perfect the ability to live in the moment (producing precisely what the moment calls for) by rehearsing closing out sets.

9) Replace the need to win with the love of the battle.

10) Reform their calmness under stress, by simulating those intense moments.

The mental and emotional strength of being a fierce competitor and a respectful human being is a learned behavior. Building mental and emotional muscle takes time and effort. The way you think and feel effects how you perform.

SPECIAL NOTE: No one can outperform their self-image. Due to their discipline, athletes like Rafa, have inner strength and inner excellence. They truly believe in themselves and their abilities because they've earned the belief.

How come so many great juniors never make it?

I've listed some of the more common road blocks you and your child will be facing in the near future. Hopefully, by now some of these key factors are being motor programmed into your psyche. View difficulties as opportunities to grow. Pressing through or around obstacles is critical!

FUN FACT: Road blocks are secret ways the game weeds out the weak. An old Japanese proverb is "fall down seven times ...get up eight."

Common Road Blocks:

Believing that if they are a better athlete, then they will win
Being a better physical athlete is only one third of the battle. If your child is weaker mentally or emotionally they will struggle. Another way to look at this issue is if an opponent looks physically superior to the rest of the field then there is most likely something missing or something broken in their mental or emotional components. If they were superior in all three, they wouldn't be in that draw.

Procrastination
Big time national titles are won by the champions because they accept the fact that they will be shedding serious blood, sweat and tears two months before the event begins. Procrastinators often do everything else except focus 100 percent on improving and fixing their problems. As long as they do not actually give 100 percent on the practice court, they will have a built in excuse..."If I had the time to practice, I could of beat her...etc."

Quantity of practices versus quality of practice

Hopefully this tip is beginning to sink in, but rallying back and forth to a hitter or even worse, having balls fed right to your child's strike zones does not in any way simulate tough playing conditions. Our battle cry is "Practice in the manner in which you are expected to perform." Remember high end tennis is not a game of catch; it is a game of keep away!

Thinking that practicing hard for one hour is enough

Top tournament play often requires that your child compete in two, best of three sets, single matches daily. Since doubles play results count for their overall ranking, throw in a doubles matches as well. Let me ask you, how many hours a day is your child expected to run their tail off?

Under training off court

If your child "thinks" that they are mostly in shape...they are most likely not in shape. Players that are in great shape know they are in great shape. Getting past the third day of a big event is going to be a challenge for every junior who only "thinks" they're in shape.

FUN FACT: Remember, solid fundamentals will get them in the draw. Being crazy fit keeps them in the draw. But being mentally and emotionally stable under stress wins titles.

Cramming last minute for an event

Peak performance requires that your child applies periodization. Cramming in training days before a national event will lead to your child's "batteries" half full. Also, their millisecond decision making skills won't be sharp. They will hesitate with their judgments and often over think under stress. Lastly, last minute crammers usually end up playing sore or injured.

Mistake management

It is essential that your child understands the difference between a "good" mistake and a "bad" mistake. Also, did the mistake stem from technical form, inappropriate "shot selections" or poor movement? Mentally making the appropriate corrections without emotional condemnation is important.

Anger management

Poor preparation is the source of the problems that cause the anger. Plans and patterns should be nurtured months before an event. Tools are sharpened and the rust is buffed out.

SPECIAL NOTE: It's not the opponent that causes the anger issues in a match. It's the fact that the opponent has exposed a weakness that wasn't fixed before the match began.

During the event, proper between point rituals and change over rituals is the key ingredient to managing emotions such as anger. Proper rituals also allow your child to save their precious physical, mental and emotional batteries needed later in the finals.

Blame management

Blaming is a common excuse many juniors prefect. Changing string tension, racquets, coaches, and academies is a short -term feel good fix. However, designing a strong personalized developmental program and sticking to it is the solution to their problems.

FUN FACT: Intermediates spend most of their time working on the strokes they already own. Advanced players spend most of their time perfecting the strokes and patterns they wish to add to their tool belt.

Lack of pre-match routines and rituals

Essential routines and rituals are used by professionals and often overlooked by junior competitors. Teens are often too cool to prepare. Rituals may include equipment preparation, nutrition and hydration at the right times, warming up their primary and secondary strokes, applying visualization sessions, going for a short run before going on the court. Champions act like champions long before they become champions.

SPECIAL NOTE: Kelly doesn't like to eat when she is nervous. So, she chose to skip breakfast before her first round match at this year's Easter Bowl. Kelly was scheduled to play at 9:30 am. The previous match went 3 long sets and Kelly didn't get on court until10:30.

Flash forward two hours and Kelly is going into the third set. Kelly had not eaten for over 16 hours! Needless to say Kelly literally ran out of gas. Not eating leads to low blood sugar. Low blood sugar leads to severe physical and mental break downs. Those break downs lead to entire emotional melt downs. Emotional melt downs lead to early losses! Kelly was out first round to a player she could have beaten blind folded. Why? She did not feel like eating.

MAKING WISER CHOICES

"Everything can be looked at from a different view."

How should my son handle cheaters?

Before we look at cheaters, let's take a quick look at your own vision. That's right, your eyes. Studies we did back in the 80's at The Vic Braden Tennis College showed some interesting data. The human eye cannot register a two millisecond event. That means you cannot actually see the ball hit the court or watch it hit your racquet. The eye is greatly affected by two variables: perspective angles and motion blur.

A. The first vision variable is the perspective angle that you're watching from. Try this eye opening exercise at home. My bet is that you'll laugh as you fail miserably.

Stand at the back fence on one side of a court. Turn facing the fence so you can't see the court. Ask a friend to place 4 balls on and just beyond the service line on the other side of the net. Ask them to repeat it with 4 new balls on the opposing baseline. When the task is complete, walk slowly to your baseline and try to make 8 correct line calls. Which balls are in, which are out?

Don't forget that in match play, the ball is only sitting there for about 2 milliseconds (two one thousands of a second). Next, walk towards the other side. As you take a sideline view things change! Now go stand behind the other baseline. Things really become clear.

We find that your child may be cheated on average 5 times a match, but usually your youngster plays out balls in even more. You see balls landing a half an inch long appear right on the line from the angle behind their own baseline. This means your child may be falling into the common trap of cheating themselves!

B. The second vision variable is motion blur. This occurs when you are running, landing, jumping etc. While in motion, your eyes are actually moving in their sockets and you could be considered "legally blind." (That's why you can't read the paper as you go for your run!) So the first time your child says, "Are you sure?" your child should be asking themselves not the opponent.

Now let's look at those Cheaters or "Creative Line Caller" from a deeper perspective. Cheaters will force your child to grow. They will stretch your child beyond their normal frustration tolerance levels. Handling cheaters is a necessary stepping stone to becoming a tennis champion.

Share with your junior champs these six factors and they will never have to worry about playing a cheater again.

Six Factors to Implement to Diffuse Cheater's Antics:

1) **Avoid Pre-Match Speculations**
   Preconceived ideas of what might happen when playing a known cheater causes so much stress that it affects the immune system and often results in players actually get sick. Many lose sleep the night before the match. Do not let your child's expectations of the possible trauma pull them away from focusing on their performance goals.

2) **Focus on What You Can Control**
   Expect about 5 bad line calls per match. This is not in your control. What is? How about the 30 unforced errors per set you commit? Limit your unforced errors to 10 per set and they can have the 5 hooks!

3) **Focus on Not Cheating Yourself**
   The truth is that most often we see players missing calls. That is, not calling out balls out! The average number of missed calls is six per match. Tighten up your own calls.

4) **Be Grateful**

Cheaters cheat because they know down deep that their skills are no match for yours. Usually a cheater is able to win because their bad calls get you so emotional that you become distracted from your performance goals and the trap is set.

NOTE: Neuroscientists call this channel capacity. The human brain cannot solve two complicated tasks at once. It is impossible to focus one's attention on performance goals and patterns while dealing with the drama of gamesmanship. A great example of channel capacity is texting and driving!

5) **Implement the Standard Procedure for Handling Cheaters First**

Begin by questioning the bad call. When that does not work, get a line judge. When the line judge leaves after a game or two, you have two options: Be an "enabler" and let the "cheater" steal the match away from you; or take matters into your own hands and fight fire with fire.

6) **Take Time to Regain Your Composer**

After a confrontation, do not begin play right away. Regain your composers first by taking a "legal" bathroom break. You will need time to get your head back into your performance goals.

FUN FACT: We conducted a seminar with 26 young national level players. We asked the ten National Champions in attendance to sit in front of the class and share their insight. The first question from Joey, a 10 year old from Las Vegas was "Were you ever forced to cheat back to stop a "cheater" from trying to steal away a National title or ITF title?

Guess how many champions answered yes, they were forced to take matters into their own hands and solve the problem? All ten!

Antic to Expect in High Level Tennis:

- Cheating on line calls (Especially on game points!)

- Accusing you of making bad line calls

- Stalling

- Changing the score

- Accusing you of changing the score

- Opponent's parents coaching

- Trying to intimidate you with their temper tantrums

- Opponent's parents doing their best to intimidate

If your child's opponents' antics become their excuses, your child is not mentally tough enough. Cheaters weed out the weak. Cheaters make champions stronger. Ask your child to play a few practice sets and allow the opponent to "hook" them a few times a set. How do they handle it?

The exercise looks like this: Every ball your youngster hits on a line, the opponent is allowed to call it out! Being mentally tough enough to handle the confrontations of a cheater is a learned behavior.

How can we help our son overcome his on-court anger?

The first thing we try to express is that not all anger is bad. Fire can be used as an analogy. Controlled fire can be used to cook meals and heat homes. Uncontrolled fire can burn down homes. Managing anger and fire requires knowledge and skill. Often it is the good anger that actually propels your child into an upward spiral. This rush of adrenaline often pushes them into a higher level. The concerns arise when the player chooses to let his or her negative emotions control their behavior. In my opinion, bad anger on the court stems from lack of knowledge, resources and tools. Here's a great example:

Johnny has only developed his primary physical strokes. His tools going into an Open tournament are his solid flat serve, his hard driving ground strokes and solid traditional volleys. We know from previous sections in this guide that secondary strokes are required in order to compete at the higher levels. Johnny draws a moonball, pusher in the second round and goes down in flames, throwing his racket as he emotionally falls apart. His fall apart is due to his lack of smart training. Without the secondary shots and patterns used to pull a great retriever out of his game, Johnny has little chance. Building the hundreds of physical, mental and emotional tools gives him solutions and plans. Now instead of getting angry he calmly shifts to plan B or C.

Below is a list of mental and emotional components your child should digest in order to begin to manage anger and stress. Talk it through and have some fun.

Developing Mental and Emotional Strength:

Say Something Good/Positive:
On the practice court, ask them to rehearse finding something they did well on each point. This will shift his focus from negative to positive. This rule applies to parents as well. Here's an example: I teach a 14 year old ranked junior that has a 128 mph serve. As he was "nailing" his serve into the box, all his father could say was, "ya, but look at his knee bend, it's pitiful...etc." Ouch!

Education is Not Completed in the Lessons:
The most important lessons are taught in tournament play. They are analyzed in match logs. Assist your child in completing a match log after each match. Match logs are great for deciphering the X's and O's of why your child is getting their results. Solutions are found in match logs.

Rehearse Successful Performance Goals Versus "I Have to Win" Goals:
You'll re-read this throughout the book over and over again! Champions are performance orientated and not outcome orientated. After a match parents need to replace "Did you win?" with "How did you play?" In the 2009 Masters Doubles, one ATP team got 81 percent of their first serves in and capitalized on 3 out of 4 break points. Guess who won easily?

Tennis is Not Fair:
There are so many reasons why this game is not fair. Understanding these issues will reduce the stress some juniors place on themselves. For instance, luck of the draw, court surfaces, match location, elements like weather (wind, sun, etc.), lucky let courts...Can you think of a few?

Everyone Gets the Same 24 Hours in a Day:
The difference is how they use it. I mentioned in a previous chapter that most juniors have an excess number of hours unaccounted for. I suggested getting a daily planner and discuss time management with your child. Assist them in organizing their on-court and off-court weekly schedule.

Managing Stress:
Experience tells us that if you are in a fight, take some time to clear your head. Get away or go for a brisk walk. Talk to your child about time management as it pertains to controlling the pace of the match. Winners often take bathroom breaks at critical times in a match, don't they? Controlling the energy flow of the match is a super way to control the fire.

Champions Experience Failure:
Discuss how most tennis champions have probably lost way more matches than your child has lost. Ambitious people experience many failures. One of my past students is Sam Querrey (ATP top 20). He's been playing full time on the ATP tour for five years. He's won five events. That means, most of the time, Sam goes home losing week in, week out. Would you say he's a loser? Not a chance!

Never Outgrow Fun:
You often see top professionals battle and still smile in the course of a match. Stress and anger clutter your thought processes, which decreases your ability to perform.

Tennis is a Gift Not a Right:
Discuss how there are millions of great athletes that are the same age as your child that will never get the opportunity to compete at this level. Tennis isn't fair, right? But has your child thought about how lucky they are to be able to play tennis and have a family that wants to support their passion?

Good Judgment Comes From Experience:
So where does experience come from? The funny answer is bad judgment. Talk to your child about how it is far less painful to learn from other peoples' failures. After a loss, stay at the tournament site and chart a top seed. Analyze others' success as well as pitfalls and learn how to avoid them.

Be Willing to Lose a Battle in Order to Win a War.
Let's say a battle is a local open tournament and a war is a top National Title. Often changing a stroke or tactical plan requires applying the new motor program before it is perfected.   Yes, they are highly likely to lose a battle or two or three. But once the new motor programs are built and they have the skills that perform well under stress, they are contenders to win the big wars.

Rehearse Ignoring their Negative Thoughts.
Ask them to allow you to video tape a few matches. As they watch the matches, ask them to count the times they had a negative thought, loss of concentration or an emotional breakdown on the court. Now, simply ask them to reduce that number each week.

Keep Your Ears Open.
Talk about listening for auditory clues. Examples are the sound of great footwork versus bad footwork, the sound of a miss-hit and amounts of spin being applied to the ball. Scan for emotional verbal signals that you or your opponent may be giving away.

The key to dissecting the opponent is playing completely engaged- eyes and ears open!

In Order to Learn They Must Pay Attention.
Ask your child to review their lesson plan with you. Ask them to teach you the 3 most important things that they worked on in their session. This kills two birds with one stone. As your child teaches you, it provides them with a deeper, clearer understanding of the topic as well as providing you with clues as to whether you are getting your money's worth in the lesson?

A Genius Simplifies the Complex.
Most lessons should be focused on "trimming the fat" off of strokes or off the players thought/focus control. Going from really good to great is not always about adding more. It is about doing less- "trimming the fat."

Stay Aggressive through the Fear.
An old saying is "courage is not the absence of fear but the ability to carry on in spite of it." Discuss how all too often we shift our style from "playing to win" to "playing not to lose." Trust me folks, they are two very different mind sets.

The Door to Success is always Marked "Push".
Ask your child if they are always pushing themselves to their fullest potential? Remind them that there are thousands of really good juniors. There are only a handful of great juniors. From a parents' perspective, if you do not push gently everyday (or pay someone to do the daily pushing) your child does not have a shot!

Most Learning Struggles Do Not Simply Disappear.
Remind your child that in most cases, ignoring the problem does not make it go away. Ignoring the issue simply limits your child's future potential. A common struggle is "How to Beat a Pusher/Retriever." Discuss how taking the right action is key. Here are some common examples of the wrong action: Changing clubs and coaches (unless they are not providing the educational environment you desire), changing racquets, changing the division lower or higher, or focusing only on hitting every ball

Harder. The correct action is developing the secondary strokes and patterns necessary to take the pusher/retrievers out of their comfort zone. Lastly, remind your child that dealing with someone angry is easier than dealing with someone silent. Everyone's scared of the unknown!

How do we spot tennis burn out?

Did you know that even the very best in the business don't stay in their "Ideal Performance State" year around? ATP and WTA tour professionals rarely play more than three events in a row. They need the critical "down" time to re-charge, heal and fix flaws.

Your child's ideal performance state lies in between the over-arousal state and the under- arousal state. Balancing that tight rope act is crucial in the ability to perform at the peak at the most important events. It's not in your child's best interest to force them to try to stay in their peak performance state 365 days a year. Taking a week off to re-charge the physical, mental and emotional batteries may help your child peak when it counts most. The number one reason why junior players report that they quit tennis or want to quit the sport is overzealous parents.

Let's look at some warning signs to assist you in spotting burn out and customizing a smarter schedule.

Spotting OVER Arousal Signs

Look for "Excessive Muscle Tension" which often leads to:

- Loss of coordination

- Reduced flexibility

- Fatigue

- Improper breathing

In turn, the "Over-Arousal State of Mind" produces:

- Reduced concentration

- Fear of failure

- Lack of emotional control

- Lack of strategy and judgment

- Poor opponent awareness

- Inability to think clearly

- Negative verbal outbursts

- Racquet banging and throwing

- Pessimism

- Stressful forced play

Coaches often say "You're over- hitting, pressing or forcing things to happen too much."

Spotting UNDER Arousal Signs

Look for lack of motivation to attend practice and/or matches. This often leads to:

- Poor equipment preparation

- Showing signs of little energy

- Appearing slow and heavy

- Poor racquet preparation

- Lack of anticipation and timing

- Negative facial expressions

- Negative body language

- Short attention span

- Eyes wondering outside the court

In turn, the "Under -Arousal State of Mind" often produces:

- Poor concentration

- Lack of concern about performance goals

- Low patience

- Lack of enthusiasm

- A sense of hopelessness

Coaches often say "you're not engaged and your mind is wondering."

One of the elements to look for in your child's matches is their emotional awareness and control. Often parents mistake being mentally tough when the issue is actually being emotionally tough.

In my opinion, if your child is showing several of the above negative signs and seems to be in a downward spiral, it may be in their best interest to put down the racquets for a while. A true contender can only stay away for a short time.

SPECIAL NOTE: During your child's time off courts, ask them to stay in physical shape by enjoying off-court training.

Is high school tennis right for my son?

Playing high school ball is a rite of passage issue. The benefits of high school tennis lean towards life experiences rather than tennis growth. There are exceptions to any rule, so let's take a deeper look at this interesting question.

The answer is a bit complicated. It greatly depends on your child's level, needs and goals. It also depends greatly on the level of the possible teammates and coaching staff at your child's high school. Some high school teams I work with are better than most college teams.

In my opinion, John Kessler is the top high school coach in the country and his team often finished the season at #1 or #2 in the nation. A player playing for John or someone like John will receive a very different high school experience than the player we will be using as an example.

Mark is a student of mine. He is a SCTA sectionally ranked player in the top 30. His national ranking is around 100. He is diligent about his tennis and spends about 15-20 hours training extremely hard every week. He has reached the semi's of three national events. His long term goals are to play for Billy Martin at his dream school UCLA.

His dad is a former player and they are certain he will play a minimum of two years on the ATP futures and challenger tours after college.

At his high school, there is one other fairly serious player on the team. The high school coach is a super nice guy. He is the biology teacher. He is coaching because he used to play high school ball and enjoys the game. (He only receives a nominal fee for coaching.)

Let's look at the POSITIVE side of high school ball for Mark and his family:

1) Plenty of court time! Mark gets to hit 3-4 hours a day.

2) Fun, peer group socialization. The van trips alone, to and from matches are a blast.

3) Wonderful team atmosphere. In such an individual sport, it's a terrific feeling to be in a gang.

4) The big fish in a small pond issue. Mark feels average participating in nationals at his ranking level. At high school he is the king! Even the cheer -leaders know him.

5) Cost: Mark's parents wrote a check for $90.00 to the booster club for the whole 4 month season.

6) Less driving to lessons and tournaments. Mark's parents don't have to worry about driving him anywhere

Now the NEGATIVE side of Mark playing high school ball:

1) Developing habits. After spending four months on court with less devoted "hobbyists", Mark develops bad work ethic issues, poor shot selection and poor mental toughness.

2) Quantity versus quality practice time. Most often Mark is goofing off with beginner/intermediate teammates or even assisting them with their games. While on the court, he's even texting friends and making plans for Friday's party.

3) Quality of match level. Mark wins 8 out of 10 matches 6-0 or 6-1

4) College scholarship factors. According to top Division 1 coaches speaking at our seminars, Coaches look at national rankings and ITF rankings. They don't consider high school ball as a High Performance Level.

5) The success formula. Remember that the success formula is spending about 20 hours of serious training every week for approximately 10 years. Is playing high school tennis for 4 months for 4 years in a row in Mark's developmental plan?

6) Rebuilding the level. It actually takes an additional 2 months of serious physical, mental and emotional training after the high school season ends to re-establish the high level Mark was playing before the season. Now,

factor in a six month loss in training time. As Mark chose to de-stress and have fun playing high school ball for 4 months. His rivals who have chosen to skip high school tennis have continued to improve.

SPECIAL NOTE: After the high school season, Mark can expect to lose to the players he use to beat handily on the USTA tournament trail.

It is important to reiterate that most high school age players are not as devoted as Mark. Others may be just as serious but need to de-compress and simply play social tennis for a season or two. If so, I recommend playing their freshman year to get a little famous at their new school and then again their senior year after they have signed their letter of intent to play for their college.

I encourage taking some time to consider all these variables. If your child is more of a "hobbyist", high school ball is one of the best experiences available. However, if your child is a phenom, a compromise may be in order. It may be best to have a meeting with the coach and/or athletic director and organize a win-win schedule. Often top players and their parents can negotiate a workable schedule.

For elite players considering high school tennis, the following three topics should be addressed (negotiated) prior to committing to the season:

1) Skipping most practice session.

2) Scheduling to only play the tougher rival matches.

3) Playing enough matches in order to qualify for the season ending state championships.

SPECIAL NOTE: In this situation, it is essential to stay alert to the common issue of the high school coach changing his mind mid-season and tearing your child down for not attending every practice, not being a team player...etc. This can have a huge negative impact on your child.

My son says I'm negative. How do I push him nicely?

Frequently, parents get fixated on what our junior "world beater" is doing wrong, what they need to change, need to learn or need to improve! Because we are so focused on our child's success, we often become preoccupied with only seeing their faults.

Focus on putting a positive spin in your approach as you gently guide your child through the "wars" of junior tennis.

Here are three ways you can apply your positive influence:

1) **Say 5 positive comments for every negative comment**. The fact is many youngsters only hear their parent's negative comments and ignore positive comments. It is important to acknowledge your child's efforts to improve.

   SPECIAL NOTE: Here's an eye opening or I should say "ear" opening trick. Place a recorder in your pocket. Record a few training sessions and self chart your positive to negative remarks!

2) **Celebrate the Positive: Reinforce what you want to see more!** The following is an example of this rule. Your son's ball toss is still too high on his serve. Instead of saying "Come on Mike…You are still tossing too high…How many stinking times do I have to tell you!" say "Hey, this is great, your toss is a lot lower. I knew you could make this easy change! Keep working and you will see your consistency really grow!"The positive approach actually gets results as you keep your relationship from getting negative and jaded.

3) **Teach Gratitude: A more positive attitude will lead to more positive behavior**. Assist your child in focusing on the good things about their life. Problems and difficulties will always be present. It is very important for your child to feel grateful about their life opportunities.

FUN FACT: There is a world of difference between "I have to play tennis today" and "I get to play tennis today." By showing gratitude, both of you will be calmer, happier and more appreciative of each other and others will want to be around you because of your positive attitudes.

To summarize, replace criticisms with a more positive approach. Hard work doesn't have to be a painful, drudgery. Yes, tennis is hard. Yes, it is a "dog-eat-dog world", but it doesn't have to be negative.

My husband wants it more than my son. Can you talk to him?

A few days after Kathy called me with her concerns, I noticed her husband Steve in the club's gym riding the life cycle. I said, "Steve, can we talk about Jake's tennis?"

"Kathy called you, didn't she?"

"Yes", I said.

He wiped the sweat off his brow and said.

"Can I meet you in the lounge in a few minutes?"

Sure, I said. I put away my tennis gear and Steve was waiting for me in the corner booth with two iced teas.

"She's upset by the way I push Jake. I know I ride him pretty damn good, but he's got a real shot."

"Steve, I agree, but what's fueling you to push him so hard?"

Steve said, *"What do you mean?"*

I said, "What's the spark that lit this tennis flame? Why is it such a life mission for you to see Jake at the top?"

Steve reaches over, shakes down two sweet-n-lows and looks down. As a coach, I can tell he's not quite sure how deep he's willing to dig. I sit in silence, giving him time and space as he drinks down half his tea.

Then he says, *"I never had a shot. I was good...real good. Man, I was better than the rich kids who were handed everything. Even back then, the kids that were ranked higher than me had one thing I didn't...parents who were invested. I wasn't born into this kind of life style. I was raised in Bloomington, Indiana. It wasn't exactly the hotbed of the tennis world back in the 70's.If you didn't play football or basketball you got beat up. Besides that, my folks couldn't be bothered. My parents weren't into sports. In fact, they weren't much into anything I did."*

You see, I loved this sport with a passion. So much that I mowed lawns in the summer and shoveled snow in the winter to buy rackets, strings, and tennis shoes. I paid my own way into any tournament I could get to. At Christmas I would ask for tennis clothes or tennis shoes or even for my folks to take me to an out of town tournament.

Hey, do you remember shoe Goo? Man, I had such big holes in the toes of my tennis shoes that I had to reapply that stuff nightly just so I wouldn't tear through all my socks. I would play until my toes bled.

These kids now-a-days have it so easy. See, my folks didn't care. It was all about them. You know how some people are givers and some are takers? Mine were takers. The only thing I remember them giving me consistently was chores!

I remember deciding back when I was a teen that when I have kids I was going to be different. I was going to give them every opportunity that I never got.

I grabbed my straw, spun the ice, drank a sip and said, "Steve, I'm sorry you didn't get your shot, I really am. But the fact is most of us didn't. Maybe that's what makes guys like you and me better parents and better coaches." I looked at him and said,

"I read once that scars are there to remind us of the past, there not here to destroy the future."

Steve finished his tea, signaled the waitress for two more and said, *"What do you recommend?"*

For the next hour or so, Steve and I devised a way for him to share his story with Jake. I thought it was meaningful for Jake to know where is father was coming from. Second, I asked Steve to let Jake share his opinion. Allow him to be the leader. Just listen with an open heart.

Third, I explained that Jake's brain type is ENFP (Extrovert, Intuitive, Feeler and Perceiver). The command and control style of military leadership that Steve grew up with doesn't work for that type. I asked Steve to let go of some of the control.

SPECIAL NOTE: When Steve was talking so openly about his parents, he didn't have a lot of positive things to say about their parenting skills, yet he adapted his father's exact parenting style.

We talked until the club closed about trying more of an inspirational leadership approach versus the drill sergeant approach. Lastly, we agreed that Steve would begin to focus on nurturing Jakes leadership skills and slowly start to teach him self reliance. Steve agreed that it's time for Jake to begin to play the game for all the right reasons.

FUN FACT: Two weeks later Kathy called me and said "Thank you so much, I don't know what you guys talked about but something clicked." Steve and Jake have a better appreciation for each other. They seem to have the same agenda but now they laugh and joke around much more. She said that Jake is actually scheduling his own practice sets, stringing his own rackets and going to the gym on his own. Steve is like a different person.

Is my child a contender or a pretender?

Here's a fun quiz. It is time to laugh a little (or cry) depending on how your child scores. Circle the self-destructive tendencies that describe your child. If you circle three or more, your child is officially pushing the boundaries of being a mentally tough contender.

Off-Court:

The Non-Committer "Mom stop nagging - I'll do it later"

The Dependent "Dad, why can't you find my hitting partners, re-grip my racquets, find my shoes, carry my bags, etc."

The T-Shirt Collector "I got in and got this cool Easter Bowl T-shirt - I'm satisfied!"

The Excuse Expert "I know the designated is tomorrow. But I have a hair appointment; I don't have time to hit!"

The Only-Play-Up Fool "I'm not playing a practice set with her. She is ranked 6 spots below me!"

The Finger Pointer "It's my parents fault, my coach's fault, my schools fault, my shoes fault, my racquets fault, etc."

The Drama Major "If I lose to her my ranking will drop, my parents will go psycho, my coach will put me in the loser group, and my friends will even think they can beat me, I'll lose my chance at my USC scholarship, I won't get the wildcard - the world will end."

The Sabotager " If I truly do everything I'm trained to do and still lose - then I'm not good enough. So I'll half train and half prepare so that if I lose, I'll have an excuse!"

The Walking Fashion Show "Maybe if I buy the latest Maria Nike dress or those Nadel shirts no one will notice I have no backhand!"

The Crabzilla " I hate this, I hate warming up, I hate eating, I hate the sun, I hate the clouds, I hate that stupid bird, I hate early matches, I hate late matches, I hate, hate, hate etc."

On-Court:

The MEGA Point Moron "Was that just - ad in? Oh…"

The River Boat Gambler "Yea, I do at least one "Tweener" a match. I made it once in practice back in 2010."

The Roller Coaster "I can plug in and play pro level tennis for 3 games, then for some reason I go unplugged and make sloppy unforced errors for 3 games in a row - now it is 3-3!

The Line Painter "I go for lines. I'm no wimpy pusher!"

The Walking Wounded "I'm too tired, my ankle hurts, I have a blister, my shoulders bugging me, I think I have the flu- is my head warm?

So, how did your child score? Does your youngster possess any of the above traits? Make this the year they start to cut out these counterproductive behaviors. Most likely these self destructive tendencies are keeping them from reaching their true potential. Is change possible? You bet! Method of thinking: "What I do now is all that matters in determining my future success. I have the power to change. I am not a slave to my past choices!"

My son watches the tennis channel all day. Is that helping?

Watching tennis on TV can be truly helpful if your child is watching with a purpose. Here are 10 categories you can ask your child to focus on while watching tennis on TV. Better yet, watch together as you both spot these ten tendencies.

1) **Watch One Player's Feet**
   Most Pros take 10 steps for every 3 steps a ranked junior takes. Have your child simply watch the shoes.

2) **Watch Between Point Rituals**
   They often appear to be looking at their strings while they use internal vision. Pros control their emotions and spot tendencies. This means they pay attention to how points are being won and lost.

3) **Spot Offense-Neutral-Defense Shot Selection**
   Way before the incoming ball reaches the net; a pro has chosen the next appropriate shot selection. Call out the correct choice as a Pro prepares to strike. If you can spot the appropriate selection with a Pro, spotting your opponents next shot will become easier.

4) **Spot This Typical Mistake: "Change the Angle ...Lose the Point"**
   Changing the angle is encouraged when you are inside the court. It is discouraged when you are behind the baseline. Watch for appropriate angle changing and inappropriate angle changing attempts. Even top pros often miss when they attempt a down the line screamer off a cross court ball from way behind the court!

5) **Spot Styles of Play**
   Who's the hard hitting baseliner? Who's the counter puncher retriever? Is there an all-court net rusher? Spotting the opponents style is the first step to devising patterns and controlling a match. If your child can spot a pros style of play, my bet is they'll be terrific at spotting their next opponents style of play!

6) **Spot Proactive Patterns**
   Pros do not simply react. They run one-two punch patterns. Can your child spot them? Ask them to point our serving patterns, return patterns, rally or net rushing shot sequences.

7) **Spot Secondary Shots**

Pros do not just have a forehand, a backhand, a serve and a volley. They have a whole "Tool Belt" full of secondary shots and they know when to activate them. Can your child spot a swing volley, a short angle/side door building shot?

8) **Watch for Open versus Closed Stance Ground Strokes**

Call out "open" and "closed" when you spot a Pro choose the appropriate stance. Understanding when and why you need them both is an important tool.

9) **Chart Errors to Winners**

Having a great understanding of where your winners and errors are coming from, as well as your opponent's winners and errors may prove to be the deciding factor if your next match goes into a tie breaker! Actually charting a pro will lead to comprehending the importance of limiting errors.

FUN FACT: Spotting the actual cause of error is the first step in error correction. The four causes of errors are: Improper technique, Reckless shot selection, Poor movement/ spacing and Poor focus/emotional control.

10) **Court Positioning Chart**

Chart a pro's winning percentage while they stay behind the baseline versus their winning percentage while going inside the court. Often, juniors think they are better from behind the baseline. After charting a match, they find their winning percentage is actually better from inside the court.

Watching tennis on TV can be a wonderful learning experience. It will secretly lead to improving your child's mental and emotional performance on the court.

What are my child's chances of going pro?

To answer this question, I have designed another fun "Pop Quiz" as a guide. (Take the quiz and you will formulate your own opinion as to what your child's chances are of becoming a Professional).

Let's assume that your child wants to play at a top Division 1 University or on the Professional Tour. They already possess keen strokes and a solid physical foundation. Now the issue is: Do their words match their actions?

<u>Simply answer each of the following question Yes or No</u>. (Then check your child's score at the end.)

Attitude

1.) Does your child possess a genuine love for the game of tennis? Yes/No

2.) Is your child being trained to be self-reliant? Yes/No

Commitment

1.) Does your child work on-court training an average of 20 hours a week? Yes/No

2.) Does your child accept that they cannot be a Champion and be a normal teenager? (They have to pick one.)Yes/No

Fitness

1.) Does your child work off -court an average of 6 hours per week on their speed, strength, flexibly, and core stability? Yes/No

2.) Does your child do exercises designed to prevent common injuries? Yes/No

Competitiveness

1.) Does your child work on how to handle frustration? Yes/No

2.) Does your child LOVE the pressure of competitive tennis? Yes/No

Confidence

1.) Is your child comfortable in stressful situations? Yes/No

2.) Does your child spend time after tournaments discovering and overcoming re-occurring nightmares? Yes/No

Problem Solving

1.) Is your child willing to overcome hardships and adversity? Yes/No

2.) Is your child able to handle the many unfair barriers of our sport? Yes/No

Focus

1.) Does your child use proper pre-match, between points, and changeover rituals? Yes/No

2.) Does your child control nervousness and distractions? Yes/No

Tactical Knowledge

1.) Does your child have well-rehearsed plans to beat the different styles of opponents? Yes/No

2.) Has your child developed two meaningful weapons? Yes/No

A Full Time Tennis Parent

1.) Is there a primary tennis parent willing to accept the responsibility, time commitment, and finances of managing a junior tennis champion's career? Yes/No

2.) Do you chart and/or video tape matches then review them with your child? Yes/No

Mental and Emotional Skills

1.) Have you begun to focus on building your child's "Tool Belt" with the mental and emotional tools that they will need to compete at the highest level? Yes/No

2.) Do you have a detailed long and short term goal list and the time management skills required to meet those goals? Yes/No

SCORING THE TEST	
0-2	Yes Answers: Relax and enjoy your normal kid.
3-5	Yes Answers: You will need a Miracle!
6-10	Yes Answers: Major changes have to be made…
11-14	Yes Answers: Your child has a serious shot at Greatness!
15-20	Yes Answers: Pack your bags for Wimbledon!

My daughter continually makes bad choices. She sabotages herself. Is this a stage she's going through?

This is a serious question with possible, deep implications. Staying on path is difficult even for the most mature teens. I can't think of a single champion who hasn't strayed "off-course" a bit. Here's a question, how long has your child been making bad choices? Has this been going on for a few weeks or a few years?

True Story: After a doubles training practice session, at the Easter Bowl Girls 14's Championship in Palm Springs, California, I took the girls out for ice cream. A young Vania King said, "No thanks, ice cream is not on my nutritional plan because I am going to be on the Pro tour." Everyone in the car laughed. Looks who is laughing now. Vania King is a Wimbledon and U.S. Open Doubles Champion!

Unfortunately, sometimes the law of attraction has negative connotations. In deeper cases, juniors form habits by continually creating a defeating negative emotional state. It, in turn, attracts a negative self-image that then attracts a cycle of negative performances.

Their words don't match their actions so there's no weight and no power behind them. Most say they want to be on the pro tour, and then choose to skip practice to go to the mall or play video games with their friends.

If your child has the talent, but needs to mature a bit, this is the section for you. Talk after dinner about each of these issues. Find out where she thinks improvement is needed. Discuss your position.

FUN FACT: National champions act like champions years before they ever win a national title. This fun fact is an example of "The Law of Attraction." The more a person creates the positive corresponding mental and emotional state, the faster they attract it and become it.

Challenge your child daily to apply the following success tools:

Encourage your player to take 100 percent responsibility for their tennis life.

- Stop blaming others or circumstances

- Give up excuses

- Give up complaints

- Avoid dramas

Reinvent an even better version of you

- Determine if tennis brings them joy, respect and purpose

- Realize they create or allow almost everything that happens to them

- Acknowledge that today's results are the result of past choices. The on-court results they achieve next month are a result of today's choices.

Believe it is possible

- Believe in and focus on their strengths

- Believe in their game

- Believing is a choice...an attitude

Manage their time

- Daily and weekly planners

- Make better choices

- Take away destructive behaviors

- Simplify positive behaviors

- Identify a proactive plan

- Try new approaches

- Acknowledge that the better choice is often the harder choice

Reinvent or stop bad habits

- Are behavioral changes needed?

- Is anyone pulling them down?

- Establishing the rules in troubled relationships

Develop a new response to bad events

- It is usually not the event that hurts; it is how they choose to respond to it.

- Identify limiting factors and find solutions

- Avoiding conflicts

- Stop negative talk: "I don't know" or "I don't care" or "I hate"

Let go of "I can't, I'm terrible, or I am not good enough"

- "I can't" reinforces a negative self-image...which in turn reinforces more negative performances

- Address difficulties as challenges and not defeats

- Continuing down the same path will get you the same results. Be open to alternative paths.

Face Fear

- Acknowledge that champions carry fear, but choose to ignore it

- FEAR is imagined

FUN FACT: The acronym for FEAR is: F = False; E= Elusions; A= Appearing; R= Real

Organize Their Goals

- List what they want, what they need to do and how they are going to get there

- Choose one singular vision

- Realize that they are the ONLY ones who can truly make this idea a reality

Change is Uncomfortable

- Release the breaks

- Go outside their comfort zone

- Welcome change

These are not necessarily tennis issues, they are life issues. If your child is having difficulties with these life tools or if discussing the issues with you, their parent, is difficult, it may be time to seek a counselor or psychologist to assist.

PARENT AND PLAYER ACCOUNTIBILITY

"Be your child's life long favorite teacher."

Does my child need mental training?

Let's first take a look at what mental training actually is. Mental, emotional training is the practical application of finding solutions to common pitfalls. We often hear, "My child has trouble closing out a 5-2 lead", "My child plays terrific in practice but horribly in matches", "My son can't beat a moonball, pusher", "My daughter can't handle cheaters!", "My son has trouble focusing for the whole match!" Mental, emotional training focuses on solving these issues.

Parents are often hesitant and a bit unclear about the role of mental or emotional training. This type of instruction involves more than simple fundamental stroke production. Developing the "hidden" skill set within your child's game is crucial for peak performance. It is a myth that only children with abnormal behavioral problems need mental or emotional guidance.

Do we have to change primary coaches to begin working on these issues?

No, not at all! A mental training coach can assist your primary coach and become a part of the team. In fact, the most intelligent coaches will encourage their players to seek out such training. It's a win-win situation for both the client and the professional. From a business stand -point, families with an actual blue print for their child's success often schedule more training sessions with their coach than ever before.

Is a lack of Mental/Emotional training holding your child back from getting the results they deserve?

TAKE THE QUIZ

The following question can be used to determine whether your child is in need of mental training. Good Luck!

1. My child plays incredible on the practice court, but often falls apart in matches. Yes/No

2. My child avoids playing practice matches every week. Yes/No

3. In matches, my child's focus is only on winning versus actual performance goals. Yes/No

4. My child doesn't apply proper change over and between point rituals in matches. Yes/No

5. My child is unorganized in planning their weekly training schedules. Yes/No

6. My child has not yet developed their secondary strokes. Yes/No

7. My child has super high expectations and expects to perform perfect every match. Yes/No

8. We haven't yet put together our entourage of hitters, teachers and trainers. Yes/No

9. My child hasn't developed plans or patterns to beat moonball pushers. Yes/No

10. My child hasn't developed plans or patterns to beat hard hitting baseliners. Yes/No

11. My child has problems managing their stress, anger and mistakes. Yes/No

12. My child hasn't yet developed their groups of proactive patterns. Yes/No

13. We do not understand or utilizes periodization training. Yes/No

14. My child has trouble dealing with external and internal distractions. Yes/No

15. My child doesn't spot mega points and mini mega points. Yes/No

16. My child doesn't know the difference between a positive mega point and a negative mega point. Yes/No

17. My child lacks confidence in his/her abilities. Yes/No

18. My child has trouble coping with cheaters. Yes/No

19. In matches, my child's mind often wonders to the past or the future. Yes/No

20. My child's training has primarily focused on stroke mechanics. Yes/No

21. My child wants to win so badly it affects his/her performance. Yes/No

22. My child freezes under stress and plays "Not to lose" instead of playing "to win." Yes/No

23. My child words ("I want to be a pro") don't match his/her actions. Yes/No

24. My child's doesn't know how to spot the opponents tendencies in match play. Yes/No

25. My child hasn't spent time identifying his/her mental game strengths and weaknesses. Yes/No

ANSWERS: If you or your child checked "Yes" to any of the above questions, you may want to consider mental and emotional training. The most important choice in developing your child's skills at the fastest rate is to have them practice in the manner in which they are expected to perform.

Peak performance under stress is not reserved for the gifted few, it's a learned behavior. Simply put, being mentally or emotionally tough under stress is a learned behavior.

Why does my child play great in practice but horrible in matches?

Friday, the day before a local junior event, John the young hitting pro carefully feeds balls waist level, in the perfect strike zone for your little Nathan. Nathan doesn't have to move and hits like a champ. On the way home, Nate says, "Man, I'm on fire! Tennis is easy! Forget the open tourney, I'm going pro!

Saturday morning rolls around and little Nate's opponent is playing "keep away" from him. He's wisely keeping balls above Nathans shoulders out of his primary strike zone. Nathan goes down in flames. After the match Nate says, "I don't get it, I was famous yesterday."

Practicing in the manner in which you are expected to perform is a battle cry heard at my workshops daily. There is a totally different set of skills that provide "competitive" confidence or confidence under stress versus simply hitting. It is important to understand that the essence of a champion doesn't simply lie in their strokes but in their head and heart. The ability to stay comfortable when things get uncomfortable is undeniably a skill. Mastering their emotions may be just the ingredient your child requires to break through to a higher level.

In typical private lessons, clinics and academies around the world the primary focus is on stroke mechanics. The attention is placed on bending your knees, change your grip, toss higher and run faster.

SPECIAL NOTE: For those of you reading the Bible from front to back, the following five topics will serve as a reminder. My effort is to provide these critical training issues a slightly different light to insure that they sink in.

No question, developing sound fundamentals is a critical element of success. However to improve your child's ability to perform under stress, it is in their best interest to switch from 100 percent stroke repetition practice to the following five practice solutions:

Practice Solutions:

- ***Stop hitting without accountability***

Hitting without accountability is like spending money with an unlimited bank account. Juniors perceive they hit better in practice because they are not aware of the sheer number of mistakes they are actually making. They remember the 10 screaming winners they hit, but forget about the 50 unforced errors they committed in the same hour.

- ***Change the focus in practice sessions***

Concentrate on skill sets such as shot selection, patterns, adapting and problem solving, spotting the opponents tendencies, tactical changes and between point rituals.

- ***Quit being a perfectionist!***

Trying 110 percent promotes hesitation, over- thinking and tight muscle contractions. Remember this topic in the blunder section? If you must worry about winning, focus on winning about 65 percent of the points. Yes, you can blow some points and allow your opponent a little glory and still win comfortably.

- ***Turn off the fear of failure***

Top players lose almost every week. Take for example one of the ATP stars I worked with as a teen, Sam Querrey. He has been on tour full time for five years. He is well adjusted, rich and famous and yet he understands that he is not going to win every tournament - which means he's ok with the fact that he will most likely lose almost every week.

- ***Replace some of the hours spent in clinics with actual matches.***

Do you want your child to learn how to play through nervousness and manage their mistakes? Do you want them to get better at closing out those 5-3 leads? Do you want them to actually beat that moonball pusher in the third set?

Players must begin to address their issues in dress rehearsal before they can expect them to win under pressure. Playing great under stress is a learned behavior. Practicing under simulated stress conditions is the solution.

The challenge is to get comfortable being uncomfortable. Rehearse doing what you're scared of doing. Take the tougher road less traveled. One of my favorite sayings is "If you want to get ahead of the pack, you can't hang in the pack."

This goes for parents as well. Obviously dropping your child off at the group lesson then going shopping for shoes is way easier than finding practice matches, charting and /or paying a college hitter to play sets. But ask yourself, is taking the convenient way out keeping your child from winning national titles?

My daughter lacks confidence. Why?

In my opinion, confidence is one of the top factors in achieving peak performance. To achieve confidence as your child progresses on her journey, it is first best to consider her goal in tennis matches. Keep in mind that the best parents and players strive for a certain type of success. That success comes in the form of performing in tournaments at the child's highest level versus having to win every match.

FUN FACT: Most junior players spend hours upon hours hitting in academies and zero hours a week in full practice matches. They've become solid ball strikers but weak competitors.

Lack of confidence issues such as self-doubt and a negative self-image arise from how athletes view past experiences. Often, when asking an adolescent what happened in the match they reply, "I don't know, I'm horrible!" Getting to the root of the issue is done by organizing tournament experiences by using match logs. Sample match logs are found later in this book!

Champions have experienced losing hundreds of times more often than your junior player. The difference is how they view it. So, how should your daughter view tournament competition? Junior tennis tournaments in general should be viewed as information gathering missions. Ask your child to complete their match logs after each real match. Share the information with your child's entourage.

How did my daughter lose her confidence?

Confidence Fades When:

- Players are not training or being trained properly.

- They are injured or sick.

- They are returning to the game after an injury or sickness.

- They have underperformed in recent competition.

- They are burnt out.

Players in a slump may be under achieving in more than one of these issues simultaneously.

How do we get her confidence back?

Rebuilding the Belief:

Confidence is a progressive spiral of positive input which leads to positive attitude. True belief and trust is earned by doing everything in your power to be the best you can be.

Let's first look deeper at ten common stepping stones that will rekindle your daughter's confidence:

1) **Re-Commit to Getting Fit**:
   Tennis specific speed, agility and stamina are key. Cross training is terrific. Hit the gym, hit the track and get physically stronger.

2) **Clear the Mind: Re-Focus on Tennis**.
   Teens can get derailed by numerous factors. School, parties, peer pressure, other sports, hobbies, shopping, etc.

3) **Proper Nutrition/Hydration**:
   What she puts in is what she gets out.
   It takes just 1-2 percent dehydration and the body is impaired mentally and physically. This could take effect with blurred vision, mental confusion, headaches, cramping etc. As for proper nutrition, the body needs high quality protein and carbohydrates at the right time to function most efficiently.

4) **Customize the Instruction**.
   Practice in the manner in which you are expected to perform." Build a game plan around exposing her great strengths while hiding her weaknesses. Customize her style to her brain and body type.

5) **Promote and Educate Independence**.
   Independent problem solving promotes confidence on and off the court. Even though some parents think they are helping, it may be wise to slowly stop doing everything for your little phenom.

6) **Surround Them with Supportive People**:
Positive coaches, trainers and friends with character are key. Is her new boyfriend pulling her focus in a new direction? Do her new friends at school want to party and shop all the time? Is her coach pessimistic or negative? This includes keeping your child away from negative or jealous tennis players or tennis parents.

FUN FACT: Girls 14's, Super Nationals Clay Court Championships in Florida. Minutes before a second round match a Southern California parent cornered my daughter, Sarah, to inform her that she is about to get killed by the next "Martina Hingis."

He practically chased Sarah to her court as he continued to banter about how unbelievable her opponent was and how she should not to feel bad about losing to this "great" player.

Luckily for us, Sarah had no idea about this second round match up. We simply told her the parent was a jealous nut and just keep the ball to the girl's pitiful backhand and we'll go to her favorite lunch spot in an hour or so.

Result: My daughter won in two straight sets and 6 years later this parent is still causing trouble on the tournament circuit.

7) **Help Others**:
Ask your daughter to assist the local food bank once a month and feed the homeless. Seeing the positive attitude of someone less fortunate reminds how fortunate they truly are!

8) **Avoid Negative Comments**:
This is any advice or stimuli that are perceived as unfavorable. The key word here is perceived. Remember this, often parents will say five positive comments and one negative ones but guess what your

child hears? Only the negative. We find that derogatory comments, tone of voice, body language or even facial expressions can tear down a sensitive player's confidence.

Examples:
A friend telling your daughter "You play Amanda next? Oh no!!! Nobody ever beats her. She won two nationals and is ranked in the top 5!"; A coach saying "You're going to run 20 laps if you miss another backhand. Just do it right!"; A parent saying after a tournament loss "You always make so many errors, maybe you should quit!"

FUN FACT: Approximately 70% of all communication is non-verbal.

9) **Proper Warm Up and Pre Match Routines**:
Confidence comes from rituals, such as, warming up all the primary and secondary strokes. This includes swing volleys, short angles, top spin lobs, proper nutrition, hydration, scouting, visualization and going for a short run before you go on the court.

10) **Perfectionists Set the Bar Too High**:
Unrealistic expectations kill confidence. Parents, just because your son won last week's tournament, don't expect him to win every one from now on. Players, a sure fire way to disable your confidence is to expect perfection. Even if you're in the zone for awhile, it's a borrowed experience. No one owns the zone. No one stays in the zone and lives there year around.

Parents, ask your player to read through these ten common confidence busters. Do any of them apply to your child? If so, customize a plan to erase them.

There's not enough time in the day, help!

My daughter can't seem to find the time to do everything needed to become a champion. Her education is the priority, so home school is out of the question. What's your advice?

In Southern California, I'm seeing most top juniors that I train spending upwards to two hours a day driving to great coaches, trainers, practice sessions, their academy and/or tournaments. A solution is "Drive Time Training". Here are a few meaningful exercises your junior player will enjoy in the car.

Drive Time Training is a great way to handle the frustrations of downtime spent in the car. Let's look into ways of educating, strength training, motivating, and visualizing while held hostage in that comfortable passenger seat.

Educating:

There is a huge variety of tennis CD's and instructional DVD's available on the market. (Visit: USPTA.org) Topics include stroke production, tactics and strategies, movement & fitness as well as our favorite the mental/emotional sides of competition. (www.tennisparentsolutions.com offers a series of junior tennis workbooks.)

Strength Training:

"How do they do strength training in a car you ask?" Most junior players lack upper body strength. Building the upper body will assist them in enjoying more powerful serves, stronger slice backhands and crisper volleys. Remember the old formula for power is:

Mass x Acceleration = Power

More importantly, training the upper body will help prevent injuries. Prevention of injuries is a critical factor in high performance tennis.

Here's How: I recommend leaving a dumbbells and bands under the passenger seat for a variety of curls, fly's and dozens of other upper body exercises.

Motivating:

Listen to motivational CD's. Some are so powerful they are literally life changing! My favorite motivators include Jack Canfield and Anthony Robbins. Check the Internet and read the reviews.

Visualization Exercises:

Turn off the radio and ask your player to close their eyes and visualize perfect primary and secondary strokes. Then the variety of their flawless patterns used to beat the different styles of opponents. Lastly, visualize walking through changeover and between point rituals. If your child has difficulties beating moonball, retrievers here's a visualization exercise. We call it mental imagery: Ask them to visualize "mock" rallies to 20 with you as you drive. Again, turn off the radio, i-Pods, video games...etc! The goal is to rehearse focusing on a single topic for a set period of time.

Try this exercise as you drive to your child's next tournament. They say hit, they then visualize a slow, high arch leaving their racket, crossing their service line, crossing the net, crossing the opponents service line bouncing pushing the opponent back. Now, the parent says hit and they repeat the visualization of the slow, high arching ball passing the opponents service line, passing the net, passing their own service line, bouncing deep on their side. Next, they say hit as the slow moonball rally continues up to twenty. If they can't focus on a pretend moonball rally, cut them some slack. My bet is that you can't either. (You'll laugh because, your mind will wonder all over the joint).

SPECIAL NOTE: If they can't focus intently on a few pretend 20 ball rallies how are they ever going to apply the actual focus skill to do it for a three hour match?

As tennis parents, it is our job to select how and when they program their minds and bodies. Positive programming to and from tennis will lead to increased knowledge, increased power, increased motivation, increased enthusiasm and increased calmness on court. Use drive time training as you shuttle back and forth.

Why should I chart matches?

- Charting matches will allow you to systematically evaluate their performance. The focus will be on their performance goals and not their outcome goals.

- Charting tournament matches is a super way to get details about the actual performance of your player. It is also a great stress buster for you.

- Charting produces important information for your child and their coaches. It provides facts versus opinions. There are dozens of types of charts. You can get as detailed or as basic as you like depending on the players age and ability level.

- Charting will identify the strengths and weaknesses of your child.

- Charting will also spot what we call "Reoccurring Nightmares". These are issues that tend to show up week after week.

FACT: It is often meaningful to chart the opponent as well.

Be aware that charts will be slightly different depending on the style of opponent your child is facing. You'll make a positive impact on your child's game by providing the coaches with the results of your findings. The Match Chart Collection is found at www.tennisparentsolutions.com)

Basic Charts to Use with Younger Champion:

Unforced Error versus Winner Chart
Young U.S. national champions generate about 10 unforced errors to 8 winners a set.

Serving Percentage Charts
First serve percentage, serving location- How often are they serving to the opponent's forehand (FH) or backhand (BH).

Type of Error Chart
Offensive, neutral, defensive shot selection errors

Cause of Error Charts
Stroke mechanics, shot selection, movement, and focus

Court Positioning Chart
Points won/lost from playing behind the court versus points won/lost playing inside the court

Mega Point Chart
The critical game points won/lost

Length of Point Chart
Points your child hits 3 balls or less versus points your child play 4 balls or more

Depth of Groundstroke Chart
This refers to where their balls are landing- Inside the service boxes versus back court

Between Point Ritual Chart
Percentages of points played after applying between point rituals versus without pre-point rituals

Service Holds and Service Breaks
Service games Won/Lost, Return games Won/Lost

Challenge your player to let go of worrying about winning and to focus on improving their charts in the upcoming year.

How would match logs help?

Match logs are simply organizational tools used to assist your youngster in understanding and critiquing their match performance. Match logs are designed to be completed by the player. Self-assessment is important. Coaches want to know how the child felt about their performance. Begin by asking your child to complete a personalized assessment of their performance after each match. Use the following match log as a blue print to customize your very own.

MATCH LOGS

Match: _____

Match Time: _____

Date: _____

Opponent_____

Ranking: _____

Conditions: _____

PREMATCH PREPARATION:

For each of the below Pre-Match Preparation details - identify the degree of accomplishment? Yes/No/Kinda (Half Effort)

1. Warm Up- 30 minutes?

2. Proper Nutrition/Hydration?

3. Stretching?

4. Visualization- 20 minutes?

5. Equipment Preparation?

6. Scouting (Live or Internet)?

7. Short Run Before Checking In?

PRE- MATCH PERFORMANCE GOALS:

The top three performance goals I will focus on today:

1. _____

2. _____

3. _____

MATCH SCORE: _____

PARENT/COACH ASSISTANCE:

1. Did they video the matches for video analysis?

2. Did they chart the match?

3. Which type of chart was used?

4. Did they de-stress or add stress to the day?

POST MATCH ANALYSIS:

Personally grade your satisfaction of your performance in the following 20 areas:

(The worst is rated 1 and the best rated is 10)

Attitude:	1 2 3 4 5 6 7 8 9 10
Effort/Fight:	1 2 3 4 5 6 7 8 9 10
Calmness	1 2 3 4 5 6 7 8 9 10
Stroke Mechanics	1 2 3 4 5 6 7 8 9 10
Shot Selection	1 2 3 4 5 6 7 8 9 10
Focus Control	1 2 3 4 5 6 7 8 9 10
Reading My Note (if Losing)	1 2 3 4 5 6 7 8 9 10
Use of Patterns	1 2 3 4 5 6 7 8 9 10
Applying Offense, Neutral, Defense	1 2 3 4 5 6 7 8 9 10
Limiting Unforced Errors	1 2 3 4 5 6 7 8 9 10
Spotting Mega Points	1 2 3 4 5 6 7 8 9 10
Attaining Performance Goals	1 2 3 4 5 6 7 8 9 10

Enjoying the Battle	1 2 3 4 5 6 7 8 9 10
Spotting Tendencies (Yours)	1 2 3 4 5 6 7 8 9 10
Spotting Tendencies (Theirs)	1 2 3 4 5 6 7 8 9 10
Self-Charting	1 2 3 4 5 6 7 8 9 10
Between Point Rituals	1 2 3 4 5 6 7 8 9 10
Mistake Management	1 2 3 4 5 6 7 8 9 10
Anger Management	1 2 3 4 5 6 7 8 9 10
Focusing on the Here and Now	1 2 3 4 5 6 7 8 9 10
Relaxing Under Stress	1 2 3 4 5 6 7 8 9 10

DISSECTING THE OPPONENT:

List the strengths and weaknesses of the opponent, as well as, their tendencies. Remember to save every match log in a folder. Your child very well may be playing the same opponent a month from now.

1. Opponent's Strengths & Weaknesses:

2. Strokes:

3. Patterns:

4. Style of Play:

5. Movement/Fitness:

6. Emotions/Fitness:

MY TOP 3 AREAS TO IMPROVE:

1. _____

2. _____

3. _____

POST MATCH PERFORMANCE:

Answer Yes, No or Kinda (Half Effort)

1. Scouting next opponent?

2. Proper nutrition and hydration?

3. Stretching?

4. Apply ice to injury?

5. Did I hit my performance goals?

NOTES:

What is a daily focus journal?

The serious contenders I know, who are finding the success they deserve are completing a Daily Focus Journal. Every night they are listing three to five things they did that day to progress their tennis career. The key words are "Every Night." Success is not a random act. It comes from a preconceived set of circumstances.

FUN FACT: Accountability builds confidence.

Examples of daily activities that could be listed in a Daily Focus Journal are:

- Playing a match

- Fixing a stroke

- Stringing their racquets

- Watching tennis on TV

- Working on between point rituals

- Working on how to beat a pusher

- Finding a new doubles partner

- Finding practice matches

- Doing 200 push ups

- Doing sprints

SPECIAL CHALLENGE: Preparing a Daily Focus Journal is very different than actually executing a Daily Focus Journal. If your child refuses to be accountable, challenge your child to document their daily activities each day for one week. At the end of one week, evaluate and discuss the challenge. What could be added or changed to their training regime? Show them their opinion counts.

Here are ten major tennis weapons as well as life lessons your child will uncover, develop and grow from if they choose to take a few moments each night as they complete their Daily Focus Journal:

1) They will learn the art of rituals

2) They will develop a work ethic

3) They will cultivate teamwork

4) They will accept self-discipline

5) They will grasp time management

6) They will appreciate self-reliance

7) They will comprehend organizational skills

8) They will get the hang of mistake management

9) They will dig deeper into managing adversity

10) They will Accept Responsibility

Winning weapons aren't only about big forehands and crushing serves. Mental and emotional skills aren't something a player is born with. They are learned behaviors. The Daily Focus Journal will require the student to be accountable for his/her actions by documenting his/her daily exercises. If your child can't be bothered documenting their successful actions, they probably won't bother to do them on a consistent basis. Accountability builds confidence.

Under achieving is usually not a result of a student's fundamental strokes but a result of the student's lack of discipline and inability to accept responsibility. Remember, tennis is a wonderful HOBBY for the part time player.

My son's words say he wants to be a pro, his actions say something else, is this normal?

Absolutely! But, the cold hard fact is that you can't be normal and be a champion. Champions are not normal, they are special. Is he willing to take a challenge? It is called The Champions Pledge. The challenge is to ask him to read this section every day for a week? This is the first step in his attempt to make his daily actions match his words.

The Real World Approach:

For decades tennis has been known to teach real world lessons. Some of these lessons are reiterated in these Champions' Pledges. After a successful junior career, college career or even after a great run on the pro tour; your child will enter the real world with these tools. These tools are needed to champion their next endeavor.

Read the below Champions Pledge together. Discuss it. Ask them to internalize it. Remind them it may prove meaningful to re-read it every few months. It is easy to look to outside sources to improve your child's results. It is even easier to blame outside sources for their lack of results. But honestly, most answers are already inside our children.

CHAMPION PLEDGES

With the below life lessons, your child will use their tools to solve their own problems on and off the court. Our greatest responsibility is teaching our children these real world lessons.

"I Pledge to Express Gratefulness"

It's a tough and lonely road towards the top. It's paved with unfair stretches of pain and heartbreak. Winning is a false and fleeting friend.

My true allies are my parents. They'll be here through thick and thin. They'll support me, listen to me and believe in me even when I've lost belief in myself. I'll remember to say thank you every day.

I'm grateful for I am one of the lucky ones. Because of them, I'm able to chase my dream. In time, with a little distance and clarity, I'll understand that very few people in this world are as lucky as I am.

"I Pledge to Complete My Daily Focus Journal"

I'm improving my confidence daily. I understand now that personal joy comes from doing everything possible to make this dream a reality. I'll survey my work each night and gladly document my achievements.

Staying on the road to success will be easy with my daily focus journal. What temptations did I resist? What stroke did I get closer to mastering? What did I do today to improve my stamina, strength and fitness? What patterns did I rehearse to beat moonball, pushers? I'm accountable to myself today and every day.

"My Words Will Match My Actions"

My words use to say "I want to be a National Champion". My actions use to say "I just want to be a Normal Teen." Transforming from a pretender to a contender is a choice.

Like the others, I despised the hard workouts, and I continually chose the easy path. I vented my frustrations and looked for the negative in each situation. Putting forth half effort became my norm.

I will transform my attitude and my work ethic. The battle is half won when I have a plan and a map for success. I will set goals and work to achieve them. Opportunities and good luck will present themselves and I will be ready.

"I Pledge to Focus My Actions"

Today's world demands that I master one thing completely. Success eludes the ones who scatter their attention, time and efforts whichever way the wind blows.

Tennis would be so much easier if I took the efforts and energy I waste on excuses and replaced those same efforts on improving.

I'm throwing myself completely into my tennis with enthusiasm. I won't hesitate and I won't procrastinate. The best in every field commit their entire being to their job. My job for now is tennis. I've cheated myself too long. I'm tired of giving less than my best.

"I Pledge to Seek Improvement in Every Loss"

The fear of failure is like a dark cloud that followed me to every match. This imaginary companion terrorized me way too long. In fact, I wouldn't even play practice matches because of the fear of failure, the fear of a loss.

There is no better tool than adversity to improve my performance next time. I need to improve certain things. This is a fact. Adversity and losses show me what to improve therefore my losses are an important part of growth.

Like a gem, I cannot be polished without friction. After the brief pain of defeat, I'll begin to erase my flaws and soon I'll be twice player I am today!

I believe my son's perfectionism is interfering with his performance. Can you help?

Assisting a perfectionist's to get the most out of their talent isn't necessarily about fixing strokes; it's about designing a new belief system. Perfectionism afflicts some of the most naturally gifted players I've ever seen. In my opinion, needing to be perfect 100 percent of the time has been a major stumbling block for those that have chosen to neglect mental training.

The Top 8 Signs you're a Perfectionist:

1) Perfectionists believe that there is only one way to do it right. After hitting a great shot, a perfectionist may say, "Yah...I hit a winner but didn't you see it? My follow through was 6.5 inches too low! Why can't I do it correctly?"

2) Perfectionists obsess over basics. Parent's often say "I can run a Fortune 500 company and control 2000 employees but I can't get my daughter to control her #@*%+... ball toss!"

3) Perfectionists love to share their inflicted disease. They not only spot their own errors but enjoy spotting yours and everyone else's flaws as well. Then, of course, they love to share it with you!

4) Perfectionists demand perfection in others. Perfectionist parent's often say to their children, "Honey, I know you're only 7 years old but you should be able to get more kick on that second serve. Dinner will wait, do another basket."

5) Perfectionists find things to worry about. Junior perfectionists often say, "What if it rains, I checked the forecast every 15 minutes last night; I could end up playing Martha if we both get to the 4th round. She's the world's biggest pusher; Or I could play Kelly, everyone knows she cheats. Remember when she cheated me in sectionals? ; Hey Dad, I heard there's a

hurricane off the coast of Florida, do you think the wind will be a factor?"…

6) Perfectionist's over- think. Due to their deep need to always be right, perfectionists often over think in matches. Teaching professionals call it paralysis by analysis. They live in their analytical left brain. This is where constant editing and judging takes place. Unfortunately for them, true "in the zone" tennis is played in the right hemisphere of the brain.

7) Perfectionists constantly second guess themselves. Junior perfectionists in a match are often thinking, "Oh, here comes a short ball, I should go in, no maybe not, it's possibly a trick, I better wait and analyze the situation, oh, look at that...too late!

8) Perfectionists often blow 5-2 leads. The match is comfortably under control and your little perfectionist misses an easy sitter. Instead of shaking it off, they blow it completely out of proportion and begin to scream and bang their racket around the court. Now, thanks' to their perfectionism, their defeated opponent sees instability and begins to believe that they can beat this crazy person. Once again, that comfortable match is now a 5-5 dog fight.

Let's begin by dissecting some of these common stumbling blocks and turn them into stepping stones:

Feeling that you must be perfect to win:
Successful tennis players are satisfied winning about 65 percent of the points in each match. Doing so allows imperfection. It also allows the opponent a little glory as they lose the match. This provides a critical distressing environment where playing at peak performance is possible.

Understanding adversity:
A good athlete is actually seeking adversity by means of a worthy opponent. You have to beat the best in order to become the best. Adversity is the challenge you seek. Adversity is not a

threat. If you have to be perfect, try being perfect in recognizing the solutions and the execution of what's needed versus focusing the perfection on the possible outcome of the match.

Controlled aggression:
Playing to win is a proactive approach to closing out those stressful situations. It's not a frantic behavior. It's a methodical attack. It's controlled aggression.

Unfortunately for most perfectionists, the fear of losing is so great that they fall into the trap of "playing not to lose.":
Pushing and playing safe is caused by fear. The fear of missing actually makes you play worse! Champions continue play "to win" when things get tight. It boils down to the development and trust in the closing phases of each game, set and match.

Unrealistic expectations:
Top nationally ranked juniors enter, on average, 30 tough tournaments a year. If they win three or four of those events, it's a great year. That mean they go home losers 26 weeks a year! Perfectionists, if you are winning 70 percent of your matches, you are ahead of the curve.

Anger:
Anger quickly comes into play when we are threatened by adversity. Angry players often make early spectators. When you play angry, you over think, shut down mentally, can't focus, heck, you can't even control muscle contractions. From a smarter perspective, view adversity as something you can learn from. Avoid anger by confronting adversity slowly with calmness, courage and positive action.

Self-Critical Behaviors:
It's ok to have a Gatorade stain on your un-tucked shirt. Your hair should be messy. Shank a few winners. Roll a few off the net tape for winners. Play slow and decrease ball speed. Give the opponent what they hate versus what you think looks like "good" tennis. Allow yourself to miss some. It doesn't have to always be pretty. Often, perfectionists would rather lose than win ugly.

Body Language:

How do you want to be perceived? Vulnerable and weak or focused and relentless? Act vulnerable and you will play vulnerable. Negative body language leads to poor performance. Act the way you want to be seen versus acting the way you feel. Use the perfectionist in you to walk, talk, think; act as if you've already won ten top events. Imagine you've already won the US Open Juniors and your just here for practice sets. The wall you chose to build around you is truly felt by others.

Focus on Executing Rituals:

Studies show that about 75 percent-80 percent of the time you're on court; you are in between points. Focus on the process of proper internal change over and between point rituals instead of results. When do those common melt downs occur? Right, in between points!

Self-Trust:

Confidence comes from trust. Trust comes from developing the four components of top level tennis. Developing the mental and emotional components is a learned behavior. Please don't expect to own these components in stressful matches if you simply don't bother to develop them. Winning those big matches comes from training outside of your normal comfort zone.

Attitude:

Understand that you choose your attitude. This means that you have the freedom to change it. Just because you've gotten negative under stress in the past doesn't mean that you HAVE to be negative in future stressful situations. If you are planning to play tennis in college, this is a major issue. I call it attitude versus aptitude. A positive attitude is what every coach is looking for. A team player with a positive attitude is a pleasure to help. A spoiled phenom with a horrible attitude is every college coach's nightmare.

Short Story: Recently one of my students, John was able to pull off a 1st round win while performing incredibly sloppy tennis. His opponent was a complete novice. Did he have a truly successful day? Not a chance. Next round, John played the #1 player in the nation. John exceeded all of his performance goals and actually played the match of his life. Even though John lost that match 6-7 in the third, he performed at a new level. Was this a successful day? You bet! Athletes cannot always control the outcome of the competition. They can control their performance levels. Champions focus on performance versus outcomes.

ON-COURT STRATEGY & TACTICS

"Dealing with someone angry is far easier than dealing with someone silent."

How do you beat a Moonball /Pusher?

No matter what you call them...retrievers, defensive baseliners, counter punchers, moonballers or pushers, at every level of junior tennis one thing is common: They have all the trophies!

In our workshops, we seek out competitors reoccurring nightmares- problems that happen over and over again. We then systematically destroy the nightmare. One nightmare that seems to be on the top of almost everyone's tennis list, around the world, is "How to Beat a Moonball Pusher." Let's look at some common key characteristics that separate most of "us" from them.

Pushers Versus the Rest of Us

- Patient versus Impatient

- Satisfied to let the opponent self-destruct versus having to hit bold winners to win

- Energy conserving versus Energy expending

- Responds after reasoning versus Responds before reasoning

- Inspired by the real/practical versus Inspired by imaginative

- Found in the present versus Found in the future

- Concerned with the task versus Concerned with the outcome and how other will view the outcome?

- Organized in their thoughts and plans versus "Uh...We will see what happens"

- Avoids surprises versus Enjoys surprises

As you can see, the psychological profile of a Pusher may be a little different than your child. Lucky for us, having a firm understanding of a pusher's brain has allowed us to organize a wonderful plan of attack!

Following are four success principles that a player must develop to be able to pull the crafty Moonball/Pusher's out of their games:

1) **Technical Strokes**

Your child must develop world class "secondary" strokes. Patterns used against a retriever consist of secondary strokes such as drop shots, short angle swing volleys...Etc.

Your child may have better "primary" strokes, but unfortunately they are little use against a pusher. It is important to understand that often good primary strokes will only work in the pusher's favor! A tool belt full of great secondary strokes needs to be developed. Often your child's "fall aparts" are caused by the lack of secondary strokes.

2) **Tactics and Strategies**

While the game continues to evolve, the foundation of strategy has not changed much over the past 100 years. For example Jack Kramer taught this theory to Vic Braden, Vic Braden taught this to me and I am passing it on to you. "If your strengths are greater than your opponent's strengths, then simply stick to your strengths. If your strengths are not as great, you must have well-rehearsed B and C plans to win the match!"

Here is an example: If your child can out "push" a world class moon ball pusher...simply pack a lunch for them and plan on a 3 hour "pushfest." If not, it may be in your youngster's best interest to develop the secondary strokes and patterns used to take a retriever out of their game. There are about six patterns that work beautifully against moon ball pushers.

3) Movement, Fitness and Strength

While lateral movement is important, the key to beating pushers lies in the forward and back directions. Here are two rhymes to help you attack moonball pushers:

"When the ball is high (defensive moonball)...Fly!"- Go (*fly*) into the court for a swing volley.

"When the ball is slow (defensive slice)...Go!" – Run (*Go*) through the volley.

Speed is broken down into two parts:

Anticipatory Speed-   Players are often incredibly fast runners, yet they are "slow as molasses" around the court. Once their anticipatory skills are developed, they begin to cover the court like a pro. Understanding vision control is a key mental issue used to develop speed. Here's one of those gems I'm going to re-visit:

As the ball travels back and forth in a point, a pro shifts his/her focus from Narrow Vision (watching the ball as it travels into their racquet) to Broad Vision (after the ball leaves their racquet) to see the big picture. Examples of broad vision include: the opponents court position, incoming strike zone, swing speed, swing length, percentage shot selection from that court position...etc.

Foot Speed- Acceleration speed, deceleration speed, recovery speed, changing of directional speed and cardio fitness obviously play a critical role in a 3 hour moon ball match. Often in a National event, your child may have to play two retrievers back to back in the same day. Pushing our players past the "Wall" is a key training tool. The wall is when your child wants to pack it up and give in.

Upper Body Strength is required because your child must be able to hit balls above their primary stroke zone. The head level strike zones (generated with top spin strokes) requires tremendous upper body conditioning and strength. Again and again, your child's emotional breakdowns stem from improper training.

4) Emotional/Focus

So as you can see, emotional "fall aparts" and lack of focus stems from a variety of key areas. Players often fall apart because they honestly are not preparing properly. Lacking in just one of these four categories is enough to lose to a retriever. We often discover that some talented athletes are lacking in all four areas. They will continue to lose to retrievers, until they choose to focus on developing these additional skill sets.

FUN FACT: A primary volley is the traditional punch volley. Secondary volleys are swing volleys, drop volleys and half volleys. Each primary stroke has secondary stroke "relatives" that also needs to mastered.

Those strategy books seem so technical. Can you make it Easy?

Strategy can be so easy yet so complicated; Strategy is changing, adapting yet ritualistic; It is science and art; It is psychological yet physical; It can be beautiful and oh so ugly; Strategy applied correctly allows your child to meet the opponent under advantageous conditions; Strategy keeps your child focused and in the correct mind set.

Let's look at strategy in a simple, yet effective format. There are three factors in understanding strategy on the tennis court. They are generic, stylistic and customized.

Generic Strategy

Generic strategy is simply applying the player's core strengths in patterns. The plan is that the opponent has to respond to your child. Create your child's patterns, plans and tactics ahead of time. Your child's generic strategy is to run their patterns and plays. Generic strategy consist of your child's favorite serving patterns, return patterns, rally patterns, short ball options and net rushing patterns.

These generic tactics will be used in January through December, from the first round through the final, In Miami or Moscow, on clay or hard courts. These are your child's everyday "nuts and bolts" game plan. The idea is to make the opponent react to them.

Stylistic Strategy

Stylistic strategy is your child's ability to adapt tactics depending on the current style of the opponent. Remind your child not to change a winning tactic just because the opponent changes game styles. A change is only made if the opponent starts to win and the momentum has switched to their side. Styles include retriever, hard hitting baseliner and all court players. It is imperative that your player develop and rehearse patterns used to beat each style of opponent.

FUN FACT: A smart competitor will change a losing style of play (shift to plan B). Has your child developed rock solid B and C game plans? The players who are winning national titles have solid B and C game plans. Rehearse all three styles of play. Encourage your child to play lesser players in practice sets. This will allow them to rehearse their B and C game plans.

Custom Strategy

Custom strategy is your child's ability to adapt to the day. Your child has to customize or adapt to different elements (wind, heat), court speeds and surfaces as well as the particular strengths and weaknesses of the current opponent.

A common word in this phase is tendencies. To borrow from the boxing world, your child needs to spot what is causing the opponent to hurt or "bleed" and then do it more. It is just as important for your child to spot what is causing their own "bleeding" and systematically stop the bleeding.

If your child is competing well in every game and often has the winning shot on his/her racquet, it is in their best interest to modify their tactics slightly while keeping the current strategic style of play. If they are losing and are not even in the points or games, a much larger shift of complete game styles may be in order. (For example: Take a bathroom break then change from a hard hitting baseliner to a steady retriever style of play.)

STRATEGY FUN FACT: The games top 3 performance goals:

1) Get 65% of your first serves in

2) Simply keep deep balls deep

3) Attack short balls

My daughter struggles with consistency. Got any tricks?

The battle cry heard daily on every court around the world is, "You need to be more consistent!" Makes sense right? It sounds simple, but how? If your child has an issue with consistency the information listed below will surely push them into a higher level.

Try the following solutions to help your daughter become a more consistent player. (Work these kinks out of your game and you'll have a house full of trophies.)

Train Almost Every Day

Practice in the manner in which you're expecting to perform. Design patterns and positions to expose your strengths and hide your weaknesses. Winning two tough matches a day for 5 days straight is the criteria for winning a national title. Try and play one match a day for a week. If it sounds too tough, try to play a full match three days straight.

Rehearse Shot Selection

The most common type of error in junior tennis is low percentage shot selection. Abiding by the laws of offence, neutral and defensive is a factor. Spotting tendencies as they occur is a critical factor in proper shot selection.

FUN FACT: The "window" your ball travels above the net is crucial in the development of depth. This is called "air zones." Consistent depth is a key to consistent wins.

Simply Match the Speed of the Incoming Ball

Champions' are comfortable matching the ball speed. Fighting the compulsion to always increase the ball speed is a sure fire way to be more consistent. When you don't have the feel in a match, shift to this plan. This is also a super warm up routine. It shows the opponent you are stable versus crazy.

Hit the Right Side of the Ball

Beginner and intermediate players are happy simply hitting the ball. Top players understand that to hit short angles, topspin lobs and slice shots, it requires more detail. The hidden gem here is that it trains you to watch the ball more carefully. You simply can't hit the outside edge of the ball traveling at you at 100 mph if you eyes are wondering.

Spacing

Proper movement and positioning around the strike zone is called spacing. Using adjustment steps to align each stroke is an underlying factor in the ability to actually use good form. A common cause of short ball errors is spacing.

Proper Form

Form includes grips, backswings, follow-throughs, core balance and keeping her head still through the strike zone. Cleaning up flawed strokes involves "trimming the fat" versus adding more to the player's stroke.

Master Spin

In high level tennis, spin is simply used as a consistency tool. The key ingredient in hitting the ball hard and in is spin. Also, as the ball speed increases in a rally, a player then must slow down the ball with spin to re-gain a positioning advantage. Controlling the point consistently is done with spin.

Repainting the Line

It is not the player's job to paint the lines. Keep balls down the center when you aren't feeling a clean groove. Players who gun for the line make boat loads of errors, allow a cheater easy access to cheat as they increase their frustration and complicate even the easiest of matches.

Increase your Fitness

Being fit has wonderful benefits. It increases your overall confidence, allows you to stay in points longer, think clearer, problem solving better, accelerate and decelerate quicker, use cleaner strokes, calm the breathing and heart rate, recover faster after long points, recover after long matches and prevent injuries.

Increase your Focus Ability

A common issue with inconsistency is playing solid, winning tennis three games in a row; then getting bored or unfocused and giving three games right back. Staying in the moment and focusing on your next point's performance goals is "key." This is done by mastering between point rituals. Also play an inner game with yourself. Focus on simply winning three points in a row when you are bored.

SPECIAL NOTE: Take a reality check. Remember charting in the last section. A great way to find out the actual cause of errors is to chart a match using the Cause of Error Chart. (www.Tennisparentsolutions.com) Ask your youngsters coach to simply chart a match or two. After an error, they place a check next to the corresponding cause.

The Four Causes of Errors:

1) Flawed Stroke/ Form

2) Shot Selection

3) Movement/ Spacing

4) Emotional/ Focus

Consistency Question: When do unforced errors or major let downs commonly occur?

- After hitting a great winner or missing a sitter, players commonly give the next point away by committing an unforced error.

- Players commonly lose their own serve right after breaking the opponent's serve.

- Players often double fault after hitting an ace.

- After winning a tight first set, players commonly play loose and find themselves down at the start of the second set.

- In tournament play, players scoring an upset victory over a higher ranked player often lose to a lesser player the very next round.

Is my daughter's style of play right for her?

I love getting questions like this at our workshops. It means the parents know what they are doing! Take a minute and think of a tennis match as a control contest.

There are three control dramas that we see in high level tennis:

1) The Power Contest

2) The Speed Contest

3) The Patience Contest

The object is to choose the contest your child performs best. Then formulate a plan to PULL the opponent into your player's world. Let's look a little deeper, yet keep it simple:

I have a top 300 WTA player training with us. Her name is Ann from Alberta, Canada. We have customized her game plan to hide her weaknesses and expose her strengths. Her body type and brain type play a major role in customizing her success.

Weaknesses

Ann is light in stature. Her opponents are generally much bigger and stronger. We checked off and excluded the "Power Contest" from her A game plan. This is not to say that she might use power as a B or C game plan. This player also has focus issues. We checked off the "Patience Contest" and excluded it as her A game plan.

Strengths

Ann possesses great speed and anticipatory skills. We chose the "Speed Contest" as her A game plan. Ann is extremely intuitive. She can sense when the opponent is vulnerable and knows "How" and "When" to move in and take away the opponents recovery and decision making time.

When this talented player chooses to play her "Speed Contest", she most often is able to move the bigger girls enough to force errors. She can also pull the pushers off the court to open up winning angles.

When Ann chooses to get into a "boomball" contest with bigger, stronger girls, she loses. When she chooses to out moonball a "World Class" moonballer she loses!

My Son is losing to players he use to beat. Can you help?

FUN FACT: The quickest way to break through a rut and go up a level is to challenge your child to focus on learning and improving versus winning. Rekindle your son's confidence by adding new tools to his game.

Ask your youngster to compete only against themselves. This is a sensational way to progress without the stress. Below I have listed three issues and provided an example for each issue:

Issue: Negative Emotional Outburst

Challenge: We have asked John to focus on reducing the sheer number of negative outburst by 25 percent each match for the next few months. The parent's role is to chart the number of times the player displays the undesired response. If he hits his mark, and decreases his negative emotional outburst by 25percent, he is a winner!

Issue: Serving Second Serves to the Opponent's Forehand.

Challenge: Stop feeding the forehand. Jenny serves 80 percent of her second serves to the opponent's strength. Her challenge is to serve 80 percent of her second serves to the opponent's weakness. The parent's role in this case is to chart each serve in match play. If Jenny can improve her second serve and place it to the opponent's weaker side, she is a winner!

Issue: Beating a Pusher

Challenge: To change the way Kelly and her dad think about Retriever/Pushers opponents. The first challenge is to assist them off the court in understanding that they are misled. They think retrievers die out in the 14's! Retrievers are the most prevalent style in women's college tennis. The second challenge is to ask the parent and the player to switch their focus to understanding and developing the patterns used to pull those crafty Retrievers out of their comfort zone.

Is the game of doubles really that important anymore?

If tennis is known as the sport of a life -time, the most popular form of tennis has to be doubles!

In Southern California, doubles can be found in the 10 and under events, all the way up to the 90 and over division. Our children will be enjoying the game of doubles way after their competitive career is over. A common thread found in senior tennis, recreational tennis, junior club teams, high school ball or even college tennis are doubles.

FUN FACT: A top woman's college coach said this about recruiting players. "In college tennis, doubles is so important, I'd much rather have a top 40 ranked player in singles with a top 30 doubles ranking any day than a top 10 singles player who has avoided playing doubles throughout their junior career."

The USTA made a critical decision a few years back. They have began combining the singles and doubles rankings into the national ranking system. This means that here in the U.S., a player's doubles results are now a very important addition to their overall National Ranking. On a monthly basis, 20 percent of the questions I now receive are doubles related questions. Below, I have listed 10 common questions along with answers and solutions:

Question: What do we look for when picking a partner?

Answer: There are a few essential elements that make a winning combination:

- Chemistry! Can they laugh and have fun winning or losing.

- Seek a partner that compliments their style. It is often called: The Hammer & Wedge System. If you are a hammer...seek a wedge.

- A common understanding of the nuances of doubles.

- Pick someone better than you.

I recommend going out to lunch and "talk shop". See if the basic personalities of all parties "gel." Some parent/coaches will only allow their child to play one style on all points regardless of the situation. This could prove disastrous. (The pro's on tour rotate their formations.) Next, play at least 2 practice matches together before committing to an event.

Question: My son is shy. He knows he should communicate to his partner during the match, but does not know what to say. What's your advice?

Answer: Doubles communication is critical in avoiding let downs and dissecting opponents. It is also important that team is synchronized; working as one. Here are some very important strategic issues that your son can use to communicate with his partner:

- The opponent's technical strokes, strengths and weaknesses.

- The opponent's favorite tactics and patterns that he has spotted.

- Identify the opponent's system of play and their likes and dislikes.

- Investigate the opponent's focus, intensity or lack of intensity.

- How to expose your team's strengths and hide your weaknesses.

- Nonverbal communication is also very important. Facial expressions, body language or even tone of voice is detectable.

SPECIAL NOTE: Between points and during change-over is when constant communication occurs. On the Pro tour, doubles partners communicate an average of 80 times a match.

Question: My 12 year old daughter is scared of doubles. She says it's confusing. Can you point her in the right direction?

Answer: Promote that doubles is a blast! It's team tennis, so she's not out there all alone. Take her to watch high school tennis matches or better yet, college ball. As you watch doubles, begin explaining the role of each position in doubles. There are unique job descriptions, patterns, positions, and tactical options in each one.

She will need to develop the tactical options for all four of these positions:

1.) The Server

2.) The Server's Partner

3.) The Return of Server

4.) The Returner's Partner

Question: My daughter will not go to the net because she says she just gets lobbed. What is she doing wrong?

Answer: Often in juniors, we see players attack the net and place their volley's back deep, right to the baseline opponent. This gives the baseline opponent plenty of time to lob.

Here's a question. Which opponent doesn't have reaction time? Is it the opposing net player or the opposing baseliner? The opposing net player is vulnerable and they can't lob effectively from that court position.

FUN FACT: The basic rule is hit long to long and short to short. That means if your daughter is back, hit to the opposing back court opponent. If your daughter is at the net, juice the opposing net girl!

Question: My son is on the court working on his strokes five days a week. He practices more than most kids ranked above him at the club. My question is why are doubles so hard for him?

Answer: Winning doubles consist primarily of serving, returning and secondary strokes. In fact, with high school age boys, the doubles points last an average of 3 hits. That is a serve, a return and maybe a volley. Practice in the method in which you are expected to perform. To be great in doubles, spend at least one day a week on serving, return of serve and transition volleys.

Question: When should a net player look to poach in modern tennis?

Answer: There are 3 basic poaching opportunities. Poaching as well as "fake" poaching is a critical element in keeping the opponents uncomfortable. Emphasize that poaching is tons of fun! Reward your child every time they attempt a poach.

FUN FACT: Often the poaching player draws errors and wins points without ever touching the ball. Visual distraction is an important element in competitive tennis. If your child needs to poach more, they should look for an opponent who is vulnerable. This could be a vulnerable court position or strike zone at contact.

SPECIAL NOTE: The primary strike zone is waist level. An opponent striking a ball around their shoe laces or leaning back to strike a ball above their shoulders puts them in a vulnerable position. So…poach!

Here are the three most common times to poach:

(For the below example, A= Server; B= Servers Partner; C= Return of Server; D=Return of Server's Partner.)

1) A serves to C's backhand= B is poaching.

2) A serves & volleys, C returns at the feet of A= D poaches.

3) A and C are in a baseline exchange, B or D spots a vulnerable strike zone, body language or court position from the opponent= poach.

Question: How are doubles different than singles?

Answer: The only true similarity is that both games are played on the same of court. Here is how we break down the differences:

- Different "secondary" technical strokes are called upon more often

- Different tactical patterns are used in different formation

- Different movement is required

- Different communication and anticipatory skills are required

SPECIAL NOTE: Plan on training doubles and/or playing doubles a minimum of one day a week.

Question: My daughter doesn't like to volley. Can she still win at doubles?

Answer: You bet! At least up to a certain level. Her first step in playing doubles without attacking the net is to choose a partner that's ok with this fact. Second, she'll need to choose a system of doubles that exposes her strengths and hides her weaknesses.

The four common systems we see on the WTA pro tour are:

1) Both players rush the net

2) One up and one back

3) Double back

4) "I" Formation

FUN FACT: The most vulnerable system in doubles is one-up-one-back. The most common system played around the world? One up one back!

Question: Our high school coach says don't ever look back at your partner's ground strokes, yet I see pro's doing it. Which is right?

Answer: In my opinion, slightly using your peripheral vision to quickly detect the quality of your partners shot is a huge advantage. Picking up visual and audible clues as soon as possible is a major part of the evolution of the game. Pros make their living by picking up these clues and moving before the opponent even makes contact with their shot. Anticipatory speed is a learned behavior.

FACT: Let's say you are at the net, only looking forward. Your partner is in trouble hitting a vulnerable, lunging floater. Well, your partner knows your dead, both opponents know your dead...Guess who does not know you're dead? ...You!

Question: My son and his partner serve 120 mph and can rip the ball. They are super aggressive, yet they lose in doubles to less talented players. What are they doing wrong?

Answer: Being aggressive in doubles is critical. Offense, unfortunately, is more than just hitting hard. Ask your son to look into the other sides of offense.

- Time management: Taking away time with aggressive positioning.

- Changing the angle of the ball versus just crushing it.

- Applying building shots: These are essential in forcing the opponent into vulnerable strike zones and positions.

How do we assist our son in decreasing his unforced errors?

All of his coaches say he is one of the most talented players they have ever seen. His form looks great. Why does he lose to less talented players?

Let's take a deeper look into the different causes of errors, starting with the mental side.

Shot selection starts with understanding that in between each shot in a rally, there is only about 2 milliseconds of actual decision making time. So, how much can you analyze in that small amount of time? The answer is not much. This means that most shot selection options are learned behaviors acquired on the practice court. That is right. These tools must be wired into a player's game way before the tournament begins. This is mental training.

To explain the importance of shot selection, we will use two of my students, **Jack** and **Jason** (brothers that couldn't be more different). Jason has chosen to focus on the mental/emotional sides of tennis early in his development, while Jack was and still is too cool to listen to this silly stuff.

Strength and Weaknesses

Situation: It is add-in. Holding serve means a comfortable 5-2 lead.

Jason: Selects to serve a big kick serve wide to the opponent's weaker side; He runs a boring, successful pattern to close out the game.

Jack: Selects to go for a huge ace down the center (the one that he made once in 2010); He misses, gets angry and rushes into a double fault.

Broad Vision

Situation: Our player just hit an offensive shot and has the opponent on the dead run, the opponent is stretching and lunging at a low slice backhand.

Jason: Spots the visual clues like the defensive court position, body language, open racket face and defensive strike zone of the opponent. He moves in, takes away the opponent's recovery time and steals an easy volley winner.

Jack: Didn't bother to learn to spot these clues, so he stands at the baseline and lets the opponent float the ball back and he re-starts the rally. Jack just missed an important opportunity to win the point.

Court Zones and Geometry

Situation: The opponent hits a deep cross-court ball.

Jason: Hits a neutral building shot 4 feet over the net and back cross court.

Jack: Tries for a screaming net skimming half volley winner down the line and creams the ball into the middle of the net.

Offense, Neutral Defensive Options

Situation: The brothers are in a vulnerable position running fifteen feet behind the baseline retrieving the opponents terrific shot.

Jason: Throws up a deep, high, defensive lob to push the opponent back and gain valuable recovery time.

Jack: Goes for an offensive, down the line pass that lands near the back fence...Then screams...AAAHHHH!

Movement, Balance and Strike Zones

Situation: Our player gets to the ball late. He is off balance and ends up striking the ball down by his socks.

Jason: Quickly dials his offensive shot selection down to neutral and elects to simply keep the opponent from taking an offensive position.

Jack: Is still in full flight and goes for a topspin rip off of his shoe laces. The ball rips into the net.

Winning Score Dynamics

Situation: Our player is winning comfortably 6-3, 4- 1.

Jason: Continues to do the exact same, boring shot selections. He closes out the match in routine fashion. He realizes the importance of saving physical and emotional energy for the next round.

Jack: Gets bored with such a lead. He begins to throw in a bunch of more exciting, yet low percentage new things. In essence, Jack has changed the shot selections that have gained him a comfortable lead. Now the set is 5-5; Jack is so angry that he is acting like a Crazy Person; throwing his racquet and yelling, "I Hate Tennis." His situation is a result of his wondering mind.

Losing Score Modifications

Situation: Our player is down 1-4 but is actually controlling the court and the points. His hard hitting baseline style is working, but he is simply missing the put away balls by a few inches.

Jason: Spots that the style is working. He adapts by staying with the hard hitting style of play and chooses to apply more top spin to his shots and simply aim three feet inside the lines.

Jack: Is so upset that he is missing, that he does not spot that fact that he is actually controlling the points with his hard hitting baseline style of play. So, he changes his hard hitting style and stands flat footed and pushes every shot. Jack's slow, short balls are now "Sitting Ducks" and the opponent has a field day hitting winner after winner. After the match, Jack says, "He was too good."

Spotting the Opponents Style Shift

Situation: Our player wins the first set 6-2. Upon the start of 2nd set, the opponent shifts from his hard hitting baseline style into a conservative, retrieving style of play.

Jason: Spots the change in style and counters by simply adapting to the "New Look." Since he is no longer receiving FREE points, Jason begins to work his selection of patterns.

Jack: Does not spot the shift in style. He begins to get frustrated by the fact that the opponent is not missing the second or third ball anymore. Without even knowing, Jack begins to play faster and hit harder. Jack is forcing winners left and right. Jack implodes once again and breaks another brand new racquet!

Elements/Environmental Conditions

Situation: The Easter Bowl (Palm Springs, Ca.) is famous for its windy conditions. Often, players have to cope with 30-40 miles per hour wind speeds. The result is that most often, cautious, consistent retriever style of play gets rewarded. The elements play a critical role in shot selection.

Jason: Adapts his offensive baseline style to a safer style of play. He looks for ways to use the wind to his advantage. He applies more spin on the ball and aims four feet inside the court on every ball. He understands that going for winners in these "crazy" conditions is an almost impossible proposition, so he buckles down and uses his "B" plan. This plan consists of letting the opponent "self-destruct."

Jack: Begins the tournament with the expectation that the conditions are unfair and he cannot play in the wind! He conveniently forgets that he has had many opportunities to practice in the wind in weeks prior to the tournament, but, he cancelled his lessons because he believed it was pointless to practice in windy conditions. (Jack lives in Southern California and Santa Ana Winds are present many times a year.)

Guess who lost first and first this year at the Easter Bowl?

Time Management

Situation: The opponent starts off on a hot streak. Within 15 minutes, he is up 4-0.

Jason: Understands that controlling and managing both sides of the net is a critical factor. Since he spots that he is clearly not in control. He takes a bathroom break. Is this legal? You bet it is! He is looking for two things to happen: One is to take enough time to actually devise a new plan of attack. Two is to act as a "Cooler." He knows that he has given the opponent's fire a chance to burn itself out. We call this a shift in momentum.

Jack: Says bathroom breaks are for "sissies." What kind of player takes a bathroom break? The answer is… smart ones!

Appropriate Short Ball Options

***Situation*:** Our Player's opponent is a terrific retriever. He positions himself 10-15 feet behind the baseline and seems to get every deep ball.

Jason: Considers the opponents preferred style. He monitors both players' court positions and elects to incorporate drop shots and short angle shots to pull the opponent out of comfort zone.

Jack: Is super talented. He can hit all four short ball options (Kill, Approach, Drop, or Side Door), but elects to simply kill every short ball as hard as he can. This plays right into his opponent's spider's web. Frustrated once again, Jack walks off the court in record time, breaking a few more racquets on the way.

Primary Versus Secondary Strokes

Situation: Our last opponent is an old school net rusher. His weapons are power and intimidation. He is coming in and everyone knows it!

Jason: Understands that simply spinning in his first serve is not as macho, but it serves a critical function: It keeps the net rusher from using the second serve as an approach shot. Also, Jason does not go for outright passing shot winners from the first pass, he resists and elects to dip the ball soft and low at the on rushing players feet. This makes the player choosing to volley earn the winning shot, while giving Jason a higher percentage shot at actually passing on the second ball.

Jack: You know Jack by now...Jack bombs away at his monster first serve. He hits his typical first serve percentage of 30 percent in. Because of the fragility of his second serve "Under Pressure", he is attacked on his second serve (70 percent of the time). The opponent quickly takes away Jack's time with his attack and breaks Jack's serve.

Like most of us, Jack is uncomfortable being attacked. He feels the pressure and goes for huge passing shots as soon as he sees the opponent begin to come in. Most of his passes land closer to the back fence than in the court. After the match Jack takes his racquet bag and shoves it into the trash can and walks to his car.

In summary, thinking, reacting, adjusting and problem solving are critical dimensions in top level tennis. Without it, the physical and technical sides of the athlete tend to drift off course. The key tools needed to compete at higher are developed by training the mental and emotional components of the game. They are rehearsed in "Live" ball practice sets.

Are you saying strokes are not important?

In a word, No. Building a solid foundation is vital to your child's success. Although this is not another "How to Stroke Book", I do have a few new insights to share on this topic!

A flawed stroke causes unforced errors, produce short vulnerable balls, cause injuries and inhibit your child's growth into the next level of competition.

FUN FACT: Strokes are a prerequisite to playing in the highest levels. Just as being tall is a prerequisite to playing in the highest levels of basketball. If just being tall earned you the right to play in the NBA, my cousin Big Vinnie wouldn't be driving a limo at Kennedy airport.

The Painter's Analogy

To this day, we can all run to the store and pick up an intermediate paint set. These pre-packaged sets come with canvas or paper, a few brushes and a strip of colored paint. These "strips" are made up of the primary colors. As we dabble and enjoy the art of painting one thing becomes evident, if only primary colors (black, brown, red, green, yellow...etc) are used, the paintings will continue to look "amateur."

Advanced artists and surely professionals have learned that to make a painting jump off the canvas, to become "life like" they need to use secondary colors as well. Now, instead of applying one shade of green, they have 12 versions of green! Advanced painters use both primary and secondary colors.

As parents, we have to encourage, educate and develop both primary and secondary stroke principles. The following are the primary and secondary strokes in a Champion tennis player's tool belt:

The Five Different Types of Forehands and Backhands are:

1.) Primary Drive

2.) High, Topspin Arch

3.) Short Angle or Side Door

4.) Slice or Drop Shot

5.) Defensive Lob

The Three Types of Serves to Develop are:

1.) Flat

2.) Kick

3.) Slice

The Four Types of Volleys to Develop are:

1.) Traditional Punch Volley

2.) Drop Volley

3.) Swing Volley/Drive Volley

4.) Half Volley

The Three Types of Lobs are:

1.) Topspin Lobs

2.) Slice Lob

3.) Re-Lob (Lobbing off of their over-head smash)

The Two Types of Overheads to Develop are:

1.) The stationary "freeze" overhead

2.) The turn & run/scissor overhead

The 6 Types of Approach Shots are:

1.) Serve and Volley

2.) Chip and Charge

3.) Drive Approach

4.) Slice Approach

5.) Drop Shot Approach

6.) Moonball Approach

FUN FACT: I got to know Tiger Woods a bit when I was the tennis director at Sherwood Country Club. We hosted his multimillion dollar charity event at Sherwood annually. Before each round of golf, Tiger practiced every club in his bag. He often, secretly, flew to the site a week or so before the actual event to rehearsing the courses uneven fairways, the speed of the greens, the feel of the sand traps and elements such as the wind. Winning is persistent preparation.

Intermediate players simply hit their primary strokes and react to whatever the opponent throws at them. Advanced players are proactive. They often run patterns used to control both sides of the net. In essence, they control both players' actions.

It takes an average of two years to develop these tools into reliable weapons. To assist your youngster in controlling the court and the match, shift focus and have some fun developing all these skills.

Before each tournament match, remind them to warm up every stroke in their bag. Winning a close tie breaker is often decided on a few points. Making that crucial swing volley versus missing it is often a matter of confidence.

PART FIVE:

QUESTIONS & ANSWERS
WITH ATP STAR
SAM QUERREY

SAM QUERREY INTERVIEW (2010)

I coached Sam in his early teens. I've witnessed him play in SCTA Open junior events, Easter Bowls, Orange Bowls, U.S. Open Juniors and now ATP tour success. The Secret weapon of the "Samurai" is his laid back, calmness on court. Experts call this frustration tolerance levels or mental toughness. (Sam was given the nickname the "Samurai" by his fans on the ATP tour)

Yes, he has a monster serve and a crushing forehand, but so do thousands of other young hopefuls. In my opinion, it's always been Sam's mental/emotional ability to control the same stress that most juniors let control them. In 2006, Sam signed a letter of intent to play college tennis for USC. He played a few pro challengers, found success and decided to give the tour a try. Once signed with SFX Sports Management, Sam made a major change. For the first time, he viewed tennis as his job. He committed. He changed his work ethic and great things began to happen.

He holds the ATP record for 10 straight aces in a win over James Blake. He won his first major title in 2008 at The Tennis Channel Open in Las Vegas. He has since won numerous titles on the ATP pro tour. In Late December, leading into the Australian Open, Sam spent the day with 10 of my nationally ranked junior players. In my opinion, the most effective learning system for most teenage boys is visual learning. So, I took them to meet Sam at UCLA. The boys watched Sam first hit with Vince Spadea (Ranked much lower than Sam on the ATP tour.)

They warmed up for about 15 minutes, played three great sets. Then Sam played a fourth set with Chase Buchanan (USTA boys 18's #1 nationally and an Ohio State standout). Then, he ran the UCLA stadium bleachers for a half an hour.

Lessons Learned:

The First Lesson- Sam warmed up quickly, played four straight sets then ran the bleachers. When was the last time your future champion did that?

The Second Lesson- The ranking and levels of the sparring partners didn't affect the quality of the session. Sam and his parents didn't say " No,no,no, we're not hitting with someone ranked 45 spots below us or with some junior!" The focus was on meeting his performance goals.

Most uneducated juniors and their parents avoid valuable practice sessions because they believe their opponent wasn't worthy of their time. The Samurai is smart and classy. He sparred with a top junior because it was beneficial to both of them. Sam was more than gracious as he answered all the players' questions, hung out with them and then went to lunch with them. It was a very memorial experience for the young players.

Sam Answered the Following Questions:

Question: What's the major difference between playing in the juniors and the pros?

Answer: In juniors you can lose focus, drop serve but then break back and still win. You can have a bad day and get away with it. In the pros, they put their foot down (play tighter with their lead) and don't let you back in!

Question: What steps did you take to become a pro?

Answer: I played national level tennis growing up, but I didn't commit to being a pro until I was 18. After I won an ATP pro challenger, I changed everything. I used to mess around a bit until then.

Question: What racquet and strings do you use?

Answer: I've been with Prince since I was 14. These are the 03 racquets. They are slightly custom weighted. The string is Luxilon 60 lbs. and Babolat gut at 64lbs.

Question: Do you modify tensions?

Answer: Yah! Depending on the elements and court surface. I'll lower or raise the tension accordingly.

Question: Tell us about your on-court training sessions?

Answer: I like to play two hours of focused tennis. You don't need to play four hours straight with a slow warm up and messing around. When I'm home I may do two sessions a day, on tour it depends on court availability and how tough my matches are...

Question: How about your off-court training?

Answer: It also depends on if I'm at a tournament or not. I do a lot of running, short sprints, squats, resistive bands. I do fly's...I don't do a lot of heavy weight lifting. My off- court training is about 1.5 hours per session.

Question: What are your eating habits?

Answer: I don't have a strict diet. I don't eat a lot of sugar though. This week, I've been having bagels, waffles and eggs for breakfast, sandwiches for lunch, steak, fish or chicken for dinner. On match days, I like pasta. During matches I'll eat a banana and I mix Gatorade with water.

Question: Are you finicky about sleep and rest?

Answer: I need 8-9 hours a night. If I don't get that much rest I get a sore throat. I'm not a nap guy. Mainly because I wear contacts and I'm too lazy to take them out. At home, I play golf and hang out with friends. On tour, I usually find something to do.

Question: Tell us about your pre-match routines?

Answer: After my warm up, I spend time listening to my i-Pod, I re-wrap my racquets and then I ride the bike to get loose. Pre-match routines vary on the tour. The Spanish guys might sprint a mile and then wet down their hair. It's up to you to find your routine.

Question: What tournaments do you like to play?

Answer: If there is an event in the U.S., I prefer that one. I get to play on center court. It's a blast! The fans are for you. I like hard courts and playing in the altitude. Clay is ok. Most guys don't like grass until they get a bit older. Pete Sampras lost in his first two Wimbledon's first round.

Question: Do you have set between point rituals?

Answer: Absolutely! I really focus on slowing down. Everyone's different, but if I'm playing poorly and losing it's because I'm rushing. I try to slow down and focus on structuring the next point. Things like, where I'm going to serve...etc. Playing at my pace is key!

Question: How do you deal with common tennis injuries?

Answer: Well, I wear these ankle braces because I sprained my ankle in 2007. The heat sleeve on my arm is because I had tennis elbow. It's preventative. I also go to the trainer when I'm on tour to get stretched and a massaged daily. It's important to get things worked on.

Question: In matches, what's your A plan and your B plan?

Answer: My A plan is pretty simple. I bomb the serve and look to jump on a forehand. My B plans varies! Sometimes it's patience, sometimes its change the spin, speed, trajectory, sometimes its serve & volley. I have multiple B plans. It's really about problem solving and adapting.

Question: How do you deal with nervousness?

Answer: Sometimes better than others. In the 08 US Open, I was in the 4th set against Rafael Nadel. I was so nervous, the crowd was going nuts, and my body was getting the chills. I had a bunch of break points. I adapted by trying to still hit hard but deep, down the middle. Sometimes it's too difficult to play. You have to fight through it. It's good to be nervous. It means you care. To beat the best guys you have to fight through nervousness.

Question: What do you work on during the off season?

Answer: Well, I came off the tour around Oct 25th. I didn't hit serves for almost six weeks. Today was the first time I went all out 100 percent on my serves. The first week back I just hit groundies. I focused on my timing and movement. I've been really focusing on my backhand, building my loop, my short angle and slice. I've also been working on spotting the short offensive ball. I'm trying to recognize it earlier. Roger Federer's the best at that.

Question: How expensive it to travel and play around the world?

Answer: Well in 2008, I play 25-30 weeks with ATP tour events, then Davis cup and exhibitions. My travel and meal expenses were well over $100,000.00. Luckily, at this level; the ATP tour picks up the hotel bill at events.

I also have my coaching fees and their meals, air travel and hotel expenses. Coaches of top 20 players earn around $100,000.00. It's not like pro basketball where the franchise pays for the coach. It comes out of the player's pocket.

At the top level, tournaments in the US provide a guarantee of around $50,000, plus 2 round trip tickets and an extra hotel room for the coach. For overseas travel, I have a travel agent. We collect points for miles and I have my coach fly economy. The tickets to the Australian Open were $8,000.00!

PART SIX:

ACCELERATING
THE LEARNING CURVE

THE TEN ESSENTIAL SKILLS

The game's standards are constantly rising. How does this affect the parent's role? Due to the increasing numbers of competitors, parents are forced to become more involved in their child's development. Even in a one-court shot gun shack tennis club in Russia, the competition is training more efficiently. The competition is bigger, faster, stronger and smarter than ever.

FUN FACT: Let's look at the evolution of the average service speed of some of the #1 player on the ATP pro tour. In 1980: Connors served 84 mph; 1990: Becker served at 112mph; 2000: Sampras served 128 mph; 2010: ATP professionals often hit the 140 mph range. Andy Roddick holds the current record with a 155mph delivery! So, what's the actual service speed your little "Joey" will need to serve on tour in the year 2020... 160 mph plus. That's evolution baby.

The evolution of your child's progress is a direct link to their new found training methods. Progress is not made while staying in one's comfort zone. I suggest asking your youngster to step outside of their comfort zone as they enter into the learning zone. This is where advances actually take place.

Let's review by isolating The Tennis Parent's Bible's ten essential steps designed to accelerate your child's performance.

NOTE: It is your job to supervise and assist in organizing the coaching staff's developmental program.

1.) BRAIN AND BODY TYPES

Hopefully, you've taken some time to visit Braintypes.com and familiarize yourself with how you and your child are wired. Different brain types certainly excel at the physical sides of the game, while some types handle pressure and evaluate tendencies better. Tennis experts agree that a combination of motor skills, mental skills and emotional skills are required at the higher levels.

Understanding your child's preferences will assist you in building their weakest link. Other wonderful benefits of understanding brain types include: disagreement resolution, relationship building, academics and vocation.

2.) ORGANIZE A QUARTERLY SCHEDULE FOR PRACTICE SESSIONS AND TOURNAMENTS

Purchase a weekly planner and structure in the different areas of development. They include off-court gym and cardio work, hitters, lessons, practice sets, and video analysis to review game days.

3.) DEVELOPING YOUR CHILD'S SECONDARY STROKES

If your child is already a competitive player their primary strokes may be developed nicely. If so, plan on spending approximately two years nurturing their secondary strokes.

4.) PRACTICE IN THE MANNER IN WHICH IN YOU ARE EXPECTATED TO PERFORM

Experience shows us that accelerated learning is within our reach. Players get the results they deserve by deliberately rehearsing their patterns. Smart players focus on fixing flaws versus ignoring them. Shift your child's workout routines from simply hitting to practicing in the manner in which they are expected to perform.

5.) NURTURING THE FOUR SIDES OF A COMPLETE PLAYER

A. Primary and Secondary Stroke Skills

The five different forehands, five different backhands, three different serves and four different volleys need to be developed. Players possessing keen primary strokes and non-existent secondary strokes are usually come in second in a field of two. Your child's game needs depth to go deep into the draw.

B. Shot and Pattern Selection Skills

Independently place your child in an offense, neutral or defensive position. Drill the movement and typical shot selections of that position. Secondly, assist your youngster in designing their proactive patterns. That is their serve patterns, return patterns, rally patterns and net rushing patterns.

C. Movement and Fitness Skills

Anticipatory speed is just as important as foot speed. A typical movement drill requires the coach to explain the sequence. The coach says, "Ok, forehand approach shot, forehand volley, backhand volley, overhead, let's do it!" I recommend training brain speed as well. So, I would say "Get to the net, I'll give you 4-6 shots". I would randomly mix in approach shots, swing volley approach shots, traditional volleys, half volleys and overheads. Now, multitasking begins. In essence, practicing in the manner in which their expected to perform.

D. **Focus and Emotional Skills**

Emotions come into play during live ball, not drills. We call it dress rehearsal/stress rehearsal. In the session, start sets half way through and asks your child to close it out with role playing.

Here are a few valuable lessons to handle in simulated live ball drills:

- If your child has trouble with cheaters, every ball your child hits on the line, the opponent gets to call it out. This rehearses emotional control, as well as the art of winning while keeping the balls away from the opponent's lines.

- If your child has trouble closing out a lead; ask them to only focus on sticking to the exact game plan that got them the lead. A common focus flaw is getting bored with an easy set, then going for low percentage, exotic shots.

- Another typical focus flaw is shifting from playing "to win" (AKA: Attacking) to simply pushing or "playing not to lose." Many intermediate players get a lead against a top seed and then begin to push. Essentially hoping the top player will choke to them, and hand them the trophy. Guess what, top players didn't reach the top by choking away matches to lesser players!

- If your child hates to play moonball/pushers, hire a college player to role play and be a pusher for the session. Ask your child to rehearse the side door/short angle pattern, the moonball approach shot to swing volley pattern and their drop shot to pass and lob patterns in actual dress rehearsals. I estimate it takes 100 hours of specific pattern rehearsals to perfect the skills needed to beat a top pusher.

6.) DEVELOP YOUR CHILD's A, B and C GAME PLANS

It is in your child's best interest to continually nurture all three styles of play. Ask them to develop and rehearse how to be a hard hitting baseliner, how to be a counter puncher/retriever as well as how to be an all court/net rusher. Most often, winning a title requires more than one game plan.

7.) CULTIVATE PROACTIVE PATTERNS

As athletes in every sport progress from recreational players to competitive players they shift from playing reactive ball to proactive. Think about organized soccer, basketball and American football. Do they run plays? You bet! In tennis, your child should shift from playing "catch" (hitting back and forth with their coach) to playing "keep away!"

8.) REHEARSE CLOSING OUT SETS

The art of winning matches lies in competitive confidence skills. As you know by now, simply hitting balls without a plan will not fuel the skills required to pull out close matches. Start practice sets at 2-2 or 3-3 and rehearse closing them out. If your child has issues closing out leads, start each practice set at 4-2. The trick is to get comfortable being uncomfortable.

9.) BETWEEN POINT RITUAL REHEARSALS

Remember that the mental and emotional breakdowns happen in between points. The solutions to those very problems also live in between points.

Ask your youngster to play sets and rehearse the thought process:

A. Get over the last point

B. Plan the next point's pattern

C. Then calmly perform their relaxation ritual

When problems arise (and they will) emotions are sure to follow. Players with emotional intelligence in the form of rituals will have the ability to cope with adversity. Focusing only on fixing the physical strokes while ignoring the emotional elements will unlikely prove effective in high level tennis.

10.) FOLLOWING YOUR CHILD'S CUSTOMIZED EVALUATION ASSESSMENT

The custom evaluation assessment will follow The Five Essential Parental Skills chapter. This will be your blue print for your youngster's accelerated learning. The evaluation section of this book is designed to assist you in adding hundreds of new tools to your child's tennis tool belt.

THE FIVE ESSENTIAL PARENTAL SKILLS

1.) ARRANGE A FINANCIAL BUDGET

Expenditures vary based on the current ability level of your child. Be careful what you wish for! As your child progresses into a higher level, so does the financial requirements.

Design a quarterly budget for rackets, strings, grips, equipment, clothes, shoes, local travel, meals, air travel, hotels, coaches, hitters, camps/academies and off-court trainers to name a few.

2.) COORDINATE A REALISTIC SCHEDULE

Customize the schedule based on your child's energy, wants and needs. At the national level, training for 4-6 hours a day, five days a week is common. Leave plenty of time to heal, recharge the batteries and always leave them wanting more.

Purchase a daily planner and design quarterly practice as well as a tournament schedule. Plan on two weeks on and one week off to fix weaknesses, improve on strengths and evaluate match logs and videotaped matches.

FUN FACT: Nothing breeds confidence you seek like winning. Often playing them down (smaller tournaments) will pump them up. Does your child get crazy nervous in a final? The experience they need to win big finals is found in smaller finals.

3.) MANAGING THE INSTRUCTORS

This includes: hitters, fundamental stroke teachers, off-court trainers and mental/emotional experts. This is an ongoing process. Each professional on your team should be given instructional goals based on your child's match logs. Set quarterly goals for each instructor.

FUN FACT: As your child enters into the top 100 in their section, switch their training routine. I suggest shifting from basic stroke production to the development of their mental and emotional skills.

4.) ESTASBLISH EXPECTATIONS

Sit down with your child and discuss your expectations. This should include performance goals such as effort, time management, nutritional requirements, perseverance and work ethic versus having to win every event they are entered into.

Review family philosophies and policies. Discuss the enforcement of such guidelines. Discuss how the goal is to eventually develop a self-reliant young adult.

FUN FACT: Many top families I work with create a family agreement statement, such as: We, the parents, agree to spend X amount of dollars quarterly as long as you (the athlete) meet the established guidelines.

5.) SYSTEMIZING THE DETAILS

Arrange the USTA tournament schedule and registration, daily logistics to and from practice sessions, training sessions as well as hotel and flight plans for national events. Monitor equipment need, nutrition and hydration needs. Manage the teaching staffs schedule and pay role.

Establish bi-weekly meetings with your child's teachers to discuss tournament issues. Be detailed, but remain flexible. The sport of tennis throws curves and you need to swerve!

Once the match begins, a player is truly on his/her own. However, prior to the actual match, the preparation, organization and developmental phases of the game requires a team effort. (See The Match Day Preparation Workbook for junior competitors at: www.tennisparentsolutions.com)

The best way to develop a world class athlete and/or a world class adult is to teach them life lessons. The above 5 Essential Skills are bigger than the game of tennis. Each skill is an essential life lesson and needed in the development of a successful adult.

PART SEVEN:

CUSTOM
SELF EVALUATION

Whether your child is a budding high school player, a USTA Open star or a National Champion this section will assist you in organizing their short and long term goals for the next year.

Reading the Tennis Bible is a prerequisite to understanding the terms and language used in this evaluation package. The custom evaluation is meant to uncover your child's strengths, weaknesses and current knowledge of the game. Then, along with your team, use this information to set a plan in motion to destroy those weaknesses.

How many tools does your child currently carry into a tournament match? Most players list a hand full. After completing this evaluation booklet, your child will uncover additional tools needed to compete at the higher levels.

STEP ONE

Step one begins by asking your child to fill out the following charts and record their personal evaluations by using the number system. The number "1" represents an extreme weakness and the number "10" represents an extreme strength. Simply note the number that best describes their comfort level.

STEP TWO

Step two is asking the primary tennis parent to circle his or her opinion of their child's confidence and ability for each topic. We often find that parents and players have a totally different view when assessing the player's strengths and weaknesses.

STEP THREE

The third step is to take any topic that either party graded a seven or below and discuss the appropriate path to improvement. I encourage you to share these evaluations, your weekly match charts and match videos, your child's match logs and daily focus journals with your coaches. The more detailed information you can provide, the shorter the learning curve.

ORGANIZING YOUR CHILD AND YOUR TEAM
(Score: 1 Extreme Weakness through 10 Extreme Strength)

1. Player/Parent Relationship   1 2 3 4 5 6 7 8 9 10

2. Player/Coach Relationship   1 2 3 4 5 6 7 8 9 10

3. Daily Nutrition/Hydration   1 2 3 4 5 6 7 8 9 10

4. Fun   1 2 3 4 5 6 7 8 9 10

5. Understanding the Parents Brain Type   1 2 3 4 5 6 7 8 9 10

6. Understanding Your Brain Type   1 2 3 4 5 6 7 8 9 10

7. Understanding Your Body Type   1 2 3 4 5 6 7 8 9 10

8. Organizing Your Game Styles   1 2 3 4 5 6 7 8 9 10

9. Spotting Opponent's Style   1 2 3 4 5 6 7 8 9 10

10. Completing Your Daily Planner   1 2 3 4 5 6 7 8 9 10

11. Independence   1 2 3 4 5 6 7 8 9 10

12. Tournament Scheduling   1 2 3 4 5 6 7 8 9 10

13. Practice Match Scheduling   1 2 3 4 5 6 7 8 9 10

14. Self-Motivation   1 2 3 4 5 6 7 8 9 10

15. Personal Work Ethic   1 2 3 4 5 6 7 8 9 10

16. Competitiveness   1 2 3 4 5 6 7 8 9 10

ORGANIZING Continued

17. Discipline   1 2 3 4 5 6 7 8 9 10

18. Accepting Responsibility   1 2 3 4 5 6 7 8 9 10

19. Self Esteem/Confidence   1 2 3 4 5 6 7 8 9 10

20. Watching Tennis Channel (Spotting   1 2 3 4 5 6 7 8 9 10
patterns & dissecting players)

List your top 3 Home Environment issues we will solve this year:

1. _____

2. _____

3. _____

OFF COURT TRAINING
(Score: 1 Extreme Weakness through 10 Extreme Strength)

1. Lateral Movement (Side to side)   1 2 3 4 5 6 7 8 9 10

2. Up & Back movement (Forward & back)   1 2 3 4 5 6 7 8 9 10

3. Aerobic Fitness   1 2 3 4 5 6 7 8 9 10

4. Ability to Accelerate   1 2 3 4 5 6 7 8 9 10

5. Ability to Decelerate   1 2 3 4 5 6 7 8 9 10

6. Speed/Agility   1 2 3 4 5 6 7 8 9 10

7. Stamina   1 2 3 4 5 6 7 8 9 10

8. Recovery Time (Between points)   1 2 3 4 5 6 7 8 9 10

9. Recovery Time (Between matches)   1 2 3 4 5 6 7 8 9 10

10. Strength (Upper body/core/lower body) 1 2 3 4 5 6 7 8 9 10

11. Body Coordination (Gross motor skills)   1 2 3 4 5 6 7 8 9 10

12. Hand-Eye Coordination (Fine motor skills) 1 2 3 4 5 6 7 8 9 10

13. Flexibility/Stretching   1 2 3 4 5 6 7 8 9 10

14. Anticipatory Speed   1 2 3 4 5 6 7 8 9 10

List your top 3 Off-Court areas to focus on this year:

1. _____

2. _____

3. _____

MATCH DAY PREPARATION

(Score: 1 Extreme Weakness through 10 Extreme Strength)

1. Equipment Preparation   1 2 3 4 5 6 7 8 9 10

2. Scouting of Opponent   1 2 3 4 5 6 7 8 9 10

3. Pre Match Visualization   1 2 3 4 5 6 7 8 9 10

4. Pre Match Warm Up Routines   1 2 3 4 5 6 7 8 9 10
   (Fundamental & Secondary shots)

5. Pre Match Run   1 2 3 4 5 6 7 8 9 10

6. Pre Match Nutrition/Hydration   1 2 3 4 5 6 7 8 9 10

7. Post-Match Stretching   1 2 3 4 5 6 7 8 9 10

8. Post-Match Nutrition/Hydration 1 2 3 4 5 6 7 8 9 10

9. Post-Match: Match logs   1 2 3 4 5 6 7 8 9 10

List your top 3 Match Day Preparation areas to focus on this year:

1. _____

2. _____

3. _____

ON COURT PHYSICAL (PRIMARY & SECONDARY STROKES)
(Score: 1 Extreme Weakness through 10 Extreme Strength)

Forehands

1. Topspin Drive   1 2 3 4 5 6 7 8 9 10

2. Topspin Loop   1 2 3 4 5 6 7 8 9 10

3. Short Angle/Side Door   1 2 3 4 5 6 7 8 9 10

4. Slice   1 2 3 4 5 6 7 8 9 10

5. Defensive Lob   1 2 3 4 5 6 7 8 910

Backhands

1. Topspin Drive   1 2 3 4 5 6 7 8 9 10

2. Topspin Loop   1 2 3 4 5 6 7 8 9 10

3. Short Angle/Side Door   1 2 3 4 5 6 7 8 9 10

4. Slice   1 2 3 4 5 6 7 8 9 10

5. Defensive Lob   1 2 3 4 5 6 7 8 9 10

Serve

1. Flat   1 2 3 4 5 6 7 8 9 10

2. Kick   1 2 3 4 5 6 7 8 9 10

3. Slice   1 2 3 4 5 6 7 8 9 10

Volley

1. Traditional Punch   1 2 3 4 5 6 7 8 9 10

2. Swing Volley   1 2 3 4 5 6 7 8 9 10

3. Half Volley   1 2 3 4 5 6 7 8 9 10

4. Drop Volley   1 2 3 4 5 6 7 8 9 10

Lob

1. Topspin Lob   1 2 3 4 5 6 7 8 9 10

2. Slice Lob   1 2 3 4 5 6 7 8 9 10

3. Re-Lob   1 2 3 4 5 6 7 8 9 10

Overhead

1. Stationary   1 2 3 4 5 6 7 8 9 10

2. Turn & Run Overhead   1 2 3 4 5 6 7 8 9 10

General Court Coverage

1. Lateral Movement (side to side)   1 2 3 4 5 6 7 8 9 10

2. Up & Back Movement (forward)   1 2 3 4 5 6 7 8 9 10

Approach Shots

1. Serve and Volley   1 2 3 4 5 6 7 8 9 10

2. Chip & Charge   1 2 3 4 5 6 7 8 9 10

3. Drive Approach   1 2 3 4 5 6 7 8 9 10

4. Slice Approach   1 2 3 4 5 6 7 8 9 10

5. Drop Approach   1 2 3 4 5 6 7 8 9 10

6. Moonball Approach   1 2 3 4 5 6 7 8 9 10

7. Steal the Volley   1 2 3 4 5 6 7 8 9 10

List your top 3 On Court Physical issues to solve this year:

1. _____

2. _____

3. _____

ON COURT EMOTIONAL
ISSUES & SOLUTIONS
(Score: 1 Extreme Weakness through 10 Extreme Strength)

1. Between Point Rituals 1 2 3 4 5 6 7 8 9 10

2. Change Over Rituals 1 2 3 4 5 6 7 8 9 10

3. Mistake Management 1 2 3 4 5 6 7 8 9 10

4. Managing Adversity & Stress 1 2 3 4 5 6 7 8 9 10

5. Controlling Your Heart Rate 1 2 3 4 5 6 7 8 9 10

6. Plan & Implement the Plan 1 2 3 4 5 6 7 8 9 10

7. Designing Proactive Patterns 1 2 3 4 5 6 7 8 9 10

8. Understanding Frustration Tolerance Level ᵴ 1 2 3 4 5 6 7 8 9 10

9. Temperament (Controlling your emotions) 1 2 3 4 5 6 7 8 9 10

10. Distraction Control 1 2 3 4 5 6 7 8 9 10

11. Quieting the Mind 1 2 3 4 5 6 7 8 9 10

12. Adapting/Problem Solving 1 2 3 4 5 6 7 8 9 10

13. Ego/Arrogance Control 1 2 3 4 5 6 7 8 9 10

14. Controlling Lapses in Concentration 1 2 3 4 5 6 7 8 9 10

15. Controlling Nervousness 1 2 3 4 5 6 7 8 9 10

16. Controlling Self Condemnation 1 2 3 4 5 6 7 8 9 10

17. Controlling "Bad" Anger 1 2 3 4 5 6 7 8 9 10

18. Limiting Unforced Errors   1 2 3 4 5 6 7 8 9 10

19. Handling Cheaters/Gamesmanship   1 2 3 4 5 6 7 8 9 10

20. Mentally Past/Present/Future   1 2 3 4 5 6 7 8 9 10

21. Mega Point Control   1 2 3 4 5 6 7 8 9 10

22. Mini Mega Point Control   1 2 3 4 5 6 7 8 9 10

23. Stopping Negative Emotional Outburst   1 2 3 4 5 6 7 8 9 10

24. Destroying Negative Beliefs   1 2 3 4 5 6 7 8 9 10

List your top 3 On Court Emotional (tactical) issues to solve this year:

1. _____

2. _____

3. _____

ON COURT MENTAL
TACTICS & STRATEGIES
(Score: 1 Extreme Weakness through 10 Extreme Strength)

1. Stroke Consistency   1 2 3 4 5 6 7 8 9 10

2. Stroke Placement   1 2 3 4 5 6 7 8 9 10

3. Mastering the Spins   1 2 3 4 5 6 7 8 9 10

4. Applying Proper Trajectories   1 2 3 4 5 6 7 8 9 10

5. Harnessing Power   1 2 3 4 5 6 7 8 9 10

6. Utilizing Zonal Tennis (Air
zones and court zones)   1 2 3 4 5 6 7 8 9 10

7. Confidence In You're A Game Plan   1 2 3 4 5 6 7 8 9 10

8. Confidence In Your B Game Plan   1 2 3 4 5 6 7 8 9 10

9. Confidence In Your C Game   1 2 3 4 5 6 7 8 9 10

10. Plan Offence/Neutral/Defensive Skills   1 2 3 4 5 6 7 8 9 10

11. Use of Percentage Shot Selection   1 2 3 4 5 6 7 8 9 10

12. The 4 Short Ball Options   1 2 3 4 5 6 7 8 9 10

13. The 4 Causes of Errors   1 2 3 4 5 6 7 8 9 10

14. The 3 Home Bases   1 2 3 4 5 6 7 8 9 10

15. Playing the Elements   1 2 3 4 5 6 7 8 9 10

16. Exposing Strengths/Hiding Weaknesses   1 2 3 4 5 6 7 8 9 10

17. Dissecting the Opponent   1 2 3 4 5 6 7 8 9 10

ON-COURT MENTAL - Continued

18. Self-Charting   1 2 3 4 5 6 7 8 9 10
     (Awareness during the match)

19. Controlling Playing Speeds   1 2 3 4 5 6 7 8 9 10

20. Attacking the One Segment Swing   1 2 3 4 5 6 7 8 9 10

21. Elongating Points   1 2 3 4 5 6 7 8 9 10

22. Beating Hard Hitting Baseliners   1 2 3 4 5 6 7 8 9 10

23. Beating Moonball/Pushers   1 2 3 4 5 6 7 8 9 10

24. Beating All Court/Net Rushers   1 2 3 4 5 6 7 8 9 10

List your top 3 On Court Mental (tactical) issues to solve this year:

1. _____

2. _____

3. _____

RANKING GOALS

	CURRENT	6 MONTH	1 YEAR
SECTIONAL			
NATIONAL			
ITF			
ATP/WTA			

CONCLUSION

First of all, I'm delighted to see that you have your parental priorities right where they should be, on your children. I'm thrilled to see that there are so many likeminded parents and coaches.

The success I've found in assisting our junior players to win 77 national singles titles is based on thousands of hours of practical application, as well as the hundreds of research studies conducted by sports educators and scientists around the world. These experts research top performers in a multitude of fields. They study how champions were raised, how often they trained and the methodology of their coaches.

I wish to thank everyone who has passed on their insight along their journey. This also includes the players, parents, the numerous tennis associations, authors, speakers, teachers, coaches, trainers and colleagues whose ideas and techniques we all share.

Remember that life and the game of tennis is always in a state of evolution. Every generation changes it, tweaks it and improves it. The games highest level is meant to be surpassed. Records are meant to be broken. One of your children will be there, breaking records set by the current crop of ATP and WTA tour professional. I'll take my hat off to you, the parent who is really the "OZ" behind the curtain.

It's with great affection that I thank the thousands of junior competitors and their families that I've had the privilege to have worked with. It's your passion that still drives me today. Through the years, many of you have thanked me, but it really should be me thanking you for the opportunity that I had to be in your lives.

Assisting young talent is thrilling. Motivating players to shift out of their comfort zone and into the learning zone is an incredible process. It's a fun, yet often, painful place for a competitive person. I really admire those willing to pay the price. Be aware, some juniors are so attached to their old ways of thinking, practicing and performing that simply training different can be quite painful in the beginning.

Please pay close attention to your child's progress and read between the lines. Encourage and praise them for their efforts. Acknowledge the struggle. Most of all, laugh a ton while enjoying the journey.

WORKSHOPS WITH FRANK GIAMPAOLO

Bring Frank and The Mental/Emotional Tennis Workshops to your Town:

1. One-on-One Private Sessions

2. High School, College Team Workshops

3. Camps, Groups & Academy Workshops

4. Tennis Parent Workshops

Workshops Include:

- Comprehensive Written Evaluation

- Customized On-Court Assessment

- Goal Setting and Assessment

- Brain and Body Type Assessment

- Preferred Learning Style Assessment

- Individual Prescription Plans

- Match Play Charting Programs

- Design and Rehearse Patterns to Expose Strengths and Hide Weaknesses

- "The Top 20 tennis Parents Blunders...and How to Avoid Them."

- Customized Scheduling to Fit Your Needs

- Build Confidence, Boost Self Esteem, and Re-Kindle Motivation

Contact: Email FGSA@earthlink.net

PARENTAL RESOURCES

Mechanics and Sport Science Books

Championship Tennis
(Frank Giampaolo (2013 1st Edition)
Human Kinetics, ISBN: 10:1450424538

Coaching Tennis Successfully, 2nd Edition
(USTA—Human Kinetics, ISBN: 0736048294

Tennis 2000,
Vic Braden & Bruns (1998) New York, Little Brown

 World Class Tennis Techniques
(Paul Roetert, Jack Groppel, Editors, Human Kinetics)

The Inner Game of Tennis, W.T. Gallwey
(1997, revised Edition)
New York Random House

Applied Sport Science for High Performance Tennis
(Crespo, Reid, Miley—ITF, ISBN: 1-903013-27-5)

Total Tennis: The Ultimate Tennis Encyclopedia
(Collins—Sport Classic Books, ISBN: 0973144343)

Maximum Tennis: 10 Keys to Releasing Your On-Court Potential
 (Saviano—Human Kinetics, ISBN: 0736042008)

Sport Psychology Books

In Pursuit of Excellence, 3rd Edition
(Orlick—Human Kinetics, ISBN: 0736031863)

Exploring Sports and Exercise Psychology
Van Raalte & Brewer (1996)
American Psychology Association.

Mental Toughness Training for Sports
(Loehr—Stephen Green Press, ISBN: 0-8289-0574-6)

Psyching for Sport: Mental Training for Athletes
(Orlick—Human Kinetics, ISBN: 0880112735)

Winning Ugly: Mental Warfare in Tennis
(Gilbert and Jamison—Fireside, ISBN: 067188400X)

Visual Tennis
(Yandell—Human Kinetics, ISBN: 0880118032)

Foundations of Sport and Exercise Psychology,
3rd Edition (Weinberg and Gould—Human Kinetics ISBN:
0736044191)

Emotions in Sport
(Hanin—Human Kinetics, ISBN: 0880118792)

Strength and Conditioning Books

Designing Resistance Training Programs
(Fleck and Kraemer—Human Kinetics, ISBN: 0736042571)

Power Tennis Training
(Chu—Human Kinetics, ISBN: 087322616X)

Core Performance
(Verstegen—Rodale Books, ISBN: 157954908X)

Strength Training Anatomy
(Delavier—Human Kinetics, ISBN: 0-7360-4185-0)

Strength Training for Young Athletes, 2nd Edition
(Kraemer—Human Kinetics, ISBN: 0736051031)

Speed Training for Tennis
(Grosser/Kraft/Schonborn—ITF, ISBN: 1-84126-030-4)

The Scientific and Clinical Application of Elastic Resistance
(Ellenbecker—Human Kinetics, ISBN: 0736036881)

College Recruiting Web Site

www.collegeboard.com Can be of assistance with their college matchmaking service.

www.collegetennisonline.com A great resource to research schools, teams, schedules current rosters, and programs.

www.NCAA.org Educate yourself on recruiting rules, course requirements and eligibility. Also where you register with the NCAA.

www.national-letter.org Questions regarding the rules and regulations of the letter of intent.

www.eligibilitycenter.org Questions regarding the rules and regulations regarding recruiting. Note: Different sports and divisions of colleges have very different rules and regulations.

www.CTORecruiting.com Post your Childs profile for college coaches to review.

E-Newsletters

Parents wishing to be added to the mailing list for the *USTA Tennis High Performance Coaching* e-newsletter or to the ITF e-newsletter should email:

e-mailsportscience@usta.com. They can also sign-up in the e-newsletter section of the High Performance websites

www.itftennis.com/coaching The ITF (International Tennis Federation) has a free monthly newsletter. You can subscribe by signing up on the ITF Coaching page.

www.TennisParentSolutions.com. The web site can link you to a free monthly Tennis Parent Newsletter.

ABOUT THE AUTHOR

Frank Giampaolo is a 25 year tennis industry veteran. He currently runs the most successful Junior Tennis Developmental Program on the West Coast. He was honored as the USPTA Southern California Tennis Director of the Year and voted a top teaching professional by Southern California Tennis & Golf Magazine year after year.

Frank founded The Tennis Parents Workshops in 1998. He has conducted workshops across the United States, Mexico, Israel, New Zealand, Australia and Canada. He founded The Mental/Emotional Tennis Workshops in the spring of 2002 and his participants have collectively won 77 National U.S. Junior Singles Championships to date.

Frank is a popular convention speaker. He is a sports educator, instructional writer for the USPTA and Tennis Magazine, Tennis View Magazine, author of Championship Tennis (Human Kinetics Publishing) and tennis researcher. His television appearances include The NBC Today Show, OCN-World team Tennis, Fox Sports, Tennis Canada and Tennis Australia.

Frank served as a tennis director of the Vic Braden Tennis College across the United States and is a United States Professional Tennis Association Certified Professional. Frank currently resides in Laguna Niguel, California.

Contact Frank Giampaolo: FGSA@earthlink.net

Enjoy the Journey, Frank

Made in United States
Orlando, FL
15 May 2022

17888036R00137